UNDERSTANDING CHILD CUSTODY

Also by Susan Neiburg Terkel

ABORTION: FACING THE ISSUES
SHOULD DRUGS BE LEGALIZED?

UNDERSTANDING CHILD CUSTODY

BY SUSAN NEIBURG TERKEL

A VENTURE BOOK
FRANKLIN WATTS   1991
NEW YORK   LONDON   TORONTO   SYDNEY

To my dear friend,
Marilyn Wise

The author gratefully acknowledges permission to reprint the following:
"Last Fragment" by Raymond Carver, *A New Path to the Waterfall,* Atlantic Monthly Press, 1989; and the Children's Bill of Rights, Dane County Family Court Counseling Service, Madison, Wisconsin.

Library of Congress Cataloging-in-Publication Data

Terkel, Susan Neiburg.
   Understanding child custody / by Susan Neiburg Terkel.
      p. cm. — (A Venture book)
   Includes bibliographical references and index.
   Summary: Describes the legal setting of custody disputes and discusses how the rights and obligations of parents and children vary under different circumstances.
   ISBN 0-531-12521-1
   1. Custody of children—United States—Juvenile literature.   2. Visitation rights (Domestic relations)—United States—Juvenile literature. [1. Custody of children 2. Visitation rights (Domestic relations) 3. Divorce.] I. Title. II. Series.
KF547.Z9T47 1991
346.7301'7—dc20
[347.30617]   90-48268   CIP   AC

CONTENTS

This book owes a great deal to the advice and suggestions of experts in this field: Carole E. Calladine, Holly Gertman, John Guidubaldi, Marcia Lebowitz, Mary E. Lindley, Hugh Ross, Betty Sherriff, Victoria Solomon, and Steve Tunstall.

Many thanks to my editor, Iris Rosoff, for her encouragement and astute judgment, and to Janet Bartlett, Alexis Gopoulos, Brooke Kowalski, Jessica Hoffman, Lee Hoffman, Carol Paull, Alison Pfeister, and Megan Russell for all their help.

My gratitude to Rick and John Hanna for letting me spread my work out at Saywells during lunchtime as well as many hours afterward.

Finally, special appreciation to my husband, Larry, and my daughter, Marni, who patiently listened to the manuscript as it progressed.

CHILDREN'S BILL OF RIGHTS

As they proceed with the process of dissolving their adult relationship, both parents recognize and acknowledge the following minimum rights of their children:

1. Right to a continuing relationship with both parents.
2. Right to be treated as an important human being with unique feelings, ideas and desires.

3. Right to continuing care and guidance from both parents.

4. Right to know and appreciate what is good in each parent without one parent degrading the other.

5. Right to express love, affection and respect for each parent without having to stifle that love because of fear of disapproval by the other parent.

6. Right to know that the parents' decision to live separately was not the responsibility of the child.

7. Right not to be a source of argument between the parents.

8. Right to honest answers to questions about the changing family relationships.

9. Right to be able to experience regular and consistent contact with both parents and to know the reason for cancellation of time or change of plans.

10. Right to have a relaxed, secure relationship with both parents without being placed in a position to manipulate one parent against the other.

Bill of Rights for Children by the staff of the Dane County Family Court Counseling Services, Madison, Wisconsin.

INTRODUCTION

And did you get what
you wanted, even so?
I did.
And what did you want?
To call myself beloved, to feel myself
beloved on the earth.

Last Fragment by Raymond Carver

All children want to feel loved. That need is as strong for those whose parents are divorcing as for those whose parents stay together.

Being loved is not all. Children want time with their parents. One of the greatest fears in children of divorce is the fear of losing contact with one of their parents. When a parent leaves home, the children miss that parent. Even years later, most children say they still miss that parent very much.

Because your divorcing parents will live apart, one or both of them will decide where you'll live and who'll be responsible for raising you. This relationship is called "having custody."

Sometimes one parent will have custody, sometimes both parents share it. If only one parent has custody, the other has the right to spend time with you. This right is called visitation.

The purpose of this book is to explain enough about custody and visitation to help you clearly understand your own situation.

1
WHAT IS CUSTODY?

When Samantha's parents told her they were getting a divorce, she wasn't surprised. "They fought all the time," Sammy said. "Long before she filed for divorce, my mother confided to me that she wanted one."

Nor was it a surprise to Sammy that her mother was asking for custody of her and her two brothers. "I knew all along we were going to stay with my mother."

Even though she was certain of the outcome, when Sammy went to court to be interviewed by a referee (someone who helps a judge), she was nervous and even a little scared. For like many other children in a similar situation, Sammy did not know what court would be like. Not really. And the unknown can be frightening.

> I went to court with my two brothers. When we got there, we were taken to a room that didn't look anything like the courtrooms I had seen in the movies or on television. It was much smaller.
>
> For half an hour, the referee asked me questions. He wanted to know who made my meals, who helped me with my homework, who disciplined me, who took me to the doctor when I was sick, things like that. Then he questioned my brothers also.

Afterwards, the referee reported back to the judge. Then the judge decided that my mother should have custody of me and my brothers, so we could still live with her.

I get along fine with my father. Since he lives a couple hours' drive from me, I don't see him too often. But we talk a lot on the telephone. And last year, he took me with him on a business trip and we had a great time.

Even though her parents divorced, Sammy still has a mother and a father. She lives with her mother and visits her father. Her mom has custody; her father has visitation. What's the difference? And can a parent without custody still be a good parent?

YOUR PARENTS ARE GETTING DIVORCED

If your parents are getting divorced, you have a lot of company. Each year, over a million children will share your plight.[1] Though some have parents who are getting divorced from their stepparent, for many children it is their parents' first divorce. And for those families, custody and visitation are major issues they must work out.

Parents divorce for many reasons. Mostly it is because they are having problems with their marriage and want a chance for a better life. Common problems include not being able to communicate anymore; not sharing enough interests or goals; having sexual problems, money problems, alcohol or drug problems; cheating; career and job pressures; disagreements over child rearing; conflicts with in-laws or other relatives; or simply feeling that the fun and excitement has left their marriage.

Sometimes both parents agree to divorce. Often, however, only one parent wants to. Yet because of our divorce laws, the other must accept that decision. And regardless of whether parents agree to divorce or only one parent wants one, children must live with the decision.

Your parents are divorcing each other. They are not divorcing you! But sometimes they are so upset and angry, so busy dealing with their own feelings, that they ignore yours. When that happens, it seems as though they have forgotten about you. This is doubtful, but nevertheless it hurts to feel that way.

Learning about custody does not take away the pain of divorce. Counseling, talking about it with others who have experienced it, even time can help do that. But learning about custody can help you see the issue more clearly. It can answer many of your questions, take away some of your uncertainty and fear, and explain why and how the legal system makes these important decisions about your personal life.

WHAT IS CUSTODY?

Custody is a legal term that simply means "who's in charge of the children." Actually, there are two aspects of custody. One is *physical custody*. This concerns your living arrangements—where you live and who takes care of you. The other is *legal custody*. Legal custody refers to the right to make decisions about you without having to consult anyone else or get the person's consent. Legal custody deals with your health, education, and welfare. For example, where you will attend school or what kind of religion you'll follow are legal-custody decisions.

When parents are married, they both have custody. And unless they abuse or neglect their children, they can take that custody for granted. That's because our laws protect the privacy of families and the right of parents to care for and make decisions about their children.

Furthermore, our society believes that all children have the right to be raised in a stable home by responsible adults. We also recognize their need to be close to those adults and to protect the closeness that is already there. These needs do not end with divorce. They are not eliminated until children grow up and can take care of themselves. That's why custody is an issue until then, and not just during a divorce.

The end of a marriage brings dramatic changes in a family. Key among them is that one household is divided into two households. Indeed, everything a couple has accumulated together during a marriage, from their house and cars to their dishes and bank accounts, must be divided between them.

However, their possessions are not all that is divided. Parenting is, too. Before their divorce, even if one parent did most of the work raising the children, they both shared the overall responsibility for their children. After the divorce, they have to divide that care and responsibility.

Where will you live? Who is going to take care of you from day to day? Who will make decisions about you? Who will be responsible for your welfare?

For your sake, your parents need to be clear about these answers. And court-ordered custody insures that they are.

Most mothers get custody, so chances are that your mother will have custody of you. But more and more mothers are sharing custody with fathers, and more and more fathers are asking for custody. And when mothers and fathers fight over custody, fathers get custody as often, if not more often, than mothers do.[2]

In order for your parents to get a divorce, they need to reach an agreement on custody and visitation.

And depending on the state where you live, your age, and your parents' situation, custody and visitation may even be a decision you get to make.

Many parents agree on custody and visitation from the start of their divorce proceedings. But most take months to reach an arrangement they can both agree on and require help from a lawyer, a social worker, or another professional to reach it. Thus, most parents are satisfied with their agreements. By the time they reach one, they have given custody and visitation a lot of thought and discussion and feel their agreement is what is best for their children (and sometimes what is best for them too).

However, not all parents *like* their agreement. It may be a compromise of what they wanted. It may be what only one parent is satisfied with. If that is the case, though, why would a parent sign an agreement he or she didn't truly like?

There are many reasons. Some parents sign in order to stop fighting over their children. Some do so because they feel so guilty about leaving and about the divorce that they don't think they deserve to get what they want. Others sign because they think they don't stand a chance of getting what they want. Still others sign to get their divorce as soon as possible, perhaps thinking that they can get what they want later (which often they can't).

Unfortunately, some parents never reach an agreement. They may be too stubborn or upset to compromise with their ex-spouse. Others simply don't know how. Though these parents are the exception, they are the ones who must turn to the courts to settle their disputes. And sometimes they turn to the courts again and again, long after their final divorce decree.

Fortunately, most parents love their children. They want to be close to them and do what is best for them.

Certainly, divorce is not what they *choose* for their children. Usually, it is a last resort, a way to manage an unsettling problem.

Despite their divorce, many parents search for ways to stay involved in their children's lives. Naturally, having custody insures that they will. But it is important to remember that your parent who is denied custody, or who agrees to let the other parent have it, *is still your parent.* Most of these parents have as much desire to stay involved as the parent with whom you live. Not all of them know how to. For it takes more effort to stay connected to children when you no longer live with them, especially if the other parent interferes with the effort.

The best custody situations are when parents have good communication, when they can put their children's interests before their own. Sadly, this doesn't always happen. Some parents honestly don't know what is good for their children. And others are too selfish to do what is right.

Custody cannot guarantee that children get raised in good homes. Nor can visitation guarantee that parents stay close to their children. But it is the way we protect children's best interests. Best interests? Our society believes that it is best for children to be raised in a home with a mother and a father. But often and for many reasons, this is not possible. Thus, what is in *your* best interest may really be in your "second-best interest."

2
CUSTODY ARRANGEMENTS

Whom will I live with? Mom or Dad? This is the question most children ask when they learn their parents are getting a divorce. And as we have already learned, for most children, the answer is Mom. But children are just as concerned about what happens to their other parent, to the one they won't live with anymore. Will I see him again? How much time will I get to spend with her? How will I stay close to him?

There is more than one kind of custody arrangement. Which kind you have depends on what your parents want or what their judge decides; what your state laws are; and what works out best for all of you.

CUSTODIAL AND NONCUSTODIAL PARENTS

Parents with physical custody are called *custodial* parents. Your custodial parent is responsible for providing you with a home and giving you day-to-day care. It is that parent's duty to make sure you eat well, have clothes to wear, get to school on time, complete your homework, and have regular checkups at the doctor and dentist.

In contrast, parents whose children don't live with them are called *noncustodial* parents. These parents visit from as little as once or twice a year to as often as several times a week. In fact, the parent may visit so often it feels like a second home to the child. A noncustodial parent may even share legal custody with a custodial parent, helping to make important decisions and contributing advice on how to raise the children.

Noncustodial is a confusing label. A parent can share legal custody, but as long as the children don't live with him, he is referred to as a noncustodial parent. Even more importantly, the label is confusing for another reason. Namely, noncustodial does not mean *non*parent. Your parent is a parent regardless of whether or not he or she has custody or whether or not you live with him or her. This is why many parents dislike the term, and many children are confused by it.

SOLE CUSTODY

Chelsea's father fell in love with someone else. Because he wanted to marry that person, he asked Chelsea's mom for a divorce. Not surprisingly, her mother was hurt, angry, and bitter. And she had no intention of sharing Chelsea with the man who had betrayed her, even if he was a good father. Furthermore, she wanted to keep Chelsea away from the other woman's influence as much as she could.

Chelsea's mother asked for custody and refused to budge on the issue. After spending months trying to persuade her to change her mind, Chelsea's father decided to avoid a court battle and went along with the arrangement. Thus, Chelsea stayed with her mother. Every other weekend, on certain holidays, and for a month during the summer, she stayed with her father.

Though Chelsea's father contributed money toward raising Chelsea, it was her mother who made all the decisions. She alone decided where Chelsea went to school, when she had to attend religious services, and what rules she was expected to follow.

When only one parent has custody, the arrangement is called *sole custody* ("sole" means one). Like Chelsea's mother, parents with sole custody have the right to make all decisions about their children without consulting the other parent. (The only exception is that in certain states the parent needs consent to move far away.) Their children live with them full time and usually visit the other parent. With sole custody, a noncustodial parent is not allowed to have his children *live* with him without a legal change in the custody arrangement.

Sole custody is the most common arrangement. One reason is tradition. Sole custody is the way custody was always awarded in the past. And traditions change slowly, especially through the legal system. Furthermore, although most states allow parents to share custody, only a few, such as California, *encourage* and prefer that parents do. Until more states follow suit, sole custody is likely to remain a popular arrangement.

There are other reasons sole custody is common. Many parents, especially fathers, don't ask for custody. This leaves the one who does—usually the mother—with custody. Why wouldn't a parent ask for custody, though? (The reason is *not* because the parent does not love the child.)

One reason is that some parents, especially those who didn't take much care of their children before a divorce, pretend that their children don't need them. Often these are the same parents who fail to make child-support or alimony payments. They may also be too wrapped up in a career or a new family to care about the children they left. When this happens, it is very painful. And usually there is little children can do about it.

Other parents are unable to care for their children. They may have problems with alcohol or drugs. They may be disabled or sick. Or they may have careers or life-styles that make custody a hardship.

Jason's father serves in the Navy, where he spends several months at a time on submarine duty. He loves and misses his son. But the only way he could have custody of Jason is to have someone else watch him, perhaps a housekeeper, his own mother (Jason's grandmother), a wife, or a girlfriend. Many fathers do rely on others to care for children in their custody. But Jason's father had none of those options. He couldn't afford a housekeeper, his mother was sick, and he didn't have a wife or girlfriend.

Often the parent who took the least physical care of the children during the marriage won't ask for custody. That's because taking care of their children, especially if they are young, overwhelms them. Or they believe that since they didn't take much care of the children before, they could never get custody now.

Some parents don't ask for custody because they can't offer as good a home as the other parent. Perhaps they can't afford to live in as safe a neighborhood or as nice a house. Perhaps they have moved, and their children prefer remaining in their old school and neighborhood.

Many parents honestly believe that sole custody is more stable and less demanding for children, or at least for *their* children. They think that living in one place and having one set of rules is better and less confusing. And though not all counselors or experts on child custody agree, many do advise their clients to ask for sole custody for these reasons.

Some parents want sole custody because they don't want to share custody. If they divorced because they couldn't get along with the other parent, they don't believe they can count on that other parent after the divorce. Or sometimes, like Chelsea's mother, they're so hurt and rejected that getting sole custody is a way to get back at and make the other parent suffer. Finally, some parents want sole custody in order to protect their children from an abusive parent.

JOINT OR SHARED CUSTODY

Increasingly, parents, judges, and child experts appreciate how important it is for children to have *each* parent involved in their lives, even if one parent is better at parenting than the other. Joint or shared custody, as it is also called, makes this possible.

When parents decide to share custody, their children take turns living with each of them. For children, this means having two homes. And if their parents don't live in the same neighborhood, it can also mean two sets of friends, and, in rare cases, even two schools.

Some children switch homes every day or two. Some divide the week, spending three or four days with each parent. Some children spend weekdays with one parent and weekends with the other. Some spend the school year with one parent and summer vacation with the other. And some children even spend alternate months, and even years, between parents.

Having two homes takes getting used to. Not everyone can adjust to this arrangement. Gretchen spent several years moving between her mother's and father's homes every three or four days. "I had two sets of everything," she said. "Two bedrooms. Two sets of clothes. It was bad. It was a time when I wanted to have a social life, have friends. You know, I'd wake up one day and say, 'Oh, my jeans are there, but my shirt's here. My book's here, but my homework is there.' I wanted to stay in one home."

On the other hand, many children say joint custody helps them remain close to both their parents. The constant moving back and forth is a hardship, but these children feel it is worth the effort. Many parents, especially those who would otherwise not have had custody, agree. And many feel it is only right. After all, you have two parents, and a divorce doesn't change that at all.

Living with a parent who shares custody may not be very different from frequently visiting a noncustodial parent. But to that parent, the difference can be great. That's because parents who share custody have an easier time than noncustodial parents do in not feeling left out of their children's lives. They feel they are as important as the other parent. Furthermore, some research studies have found that this helps parents be more willing to pay child support and accept more responsibility for their children. Most of all, it helps them stay involved in their children's lives.

JOINT LEGAL CUSTODY

Sometimes it is not possible for parents to share physical custody. And sometimes children refuse to cooperate. In those cases, parents can still share legal custody.

Heather lived with her mom. Her dad lived far away and saw her only twice a year, at Thanksgiving and during summer vacation. They talked often on the telephone to try to make up for the distance. When it was time to decide whether or not Heather should be confirmed, her mom discussed it with her dad. Together they decided that it would be a good experience for Heather.

Even if they didn't share custody, Heather's mom could still have discussed the matter with Heather's dad. But because they did share custody, being part of the decision wasn't her mom's choice; it was her dad's legal right.

After his parents' divorce, Ryan was so upset he

had trouble concentrating on his schoolwork. His slipping grades concerned his father. Yet when his father called school to see Ryan's records, he was told that without legal custody he could not see them. Ryan's father was not only frustrated, he felt left out. If he had shared legal custody, his frustration might have been spared.

Sharing custody gives noncustodial parents more rights. It allows them to participate in decisions about their children's education, religion, and welfare. Moreover, it helps parents who lose physical custody feel less like "losers." Sharing legal custody keeps parents feeling worthwhile in their children's lives. In turn, they are more willing to be a part of their children's lives.

Not everyone agrees that joint legal custody works. Some people believe that joint legal custody keeps the parents fighting in their children's lives, and gives unreasonable parents too much control.

DOVE-NESTING

Patrick's parents have joint custody. Instead of Patrick going back and forth between his parents' homes, his parents decided it was better for Patrick and his brother to remain in the house where they grew up. Their mother and father moved out and lived elsewhere, in separate homes. Then they took turns living with Patrick and his brother. That way, it was Patrick's parents, not him or his brother, doing the moving, yet his parents were still able to share custody.

Dove-nesting, as this type of custody is called, is rare and usually only temporary. One reason for this is that lives change, and dove-nesting is living in the past. It is also very expensive to maintain a separate household for children. Thus, only very wealthy parents can usually afford to try this type of arrangement.

SPLIT CUSTODY

Another form of joint custody is *split custody*. (Split custody is also a description for splitting brothers and sisters between parents.) Split custody is a cross between sole and joint custody. Instead of sharing custody, parents take turns having sole custody.

Josh and his sister Kelly have a split-custody arrangement. During even-numbered years, Josh and Kelly live with their father in Santa Fe, New Mexico. During odd-numbered years, they live in Seattle, Washington, with their mother.

For parents who cannot agree or who prefer to be independent of each other, split custody is an option. It also gives custody, if only part-time, to parents who might otherwise not have had it.

WHICH IS BETTER?

An important debate is going on about joint and sole custody. Namely, which arrangement is better?

Many experts agree that if parents get along (joint custody works best with good communication between the parties), and if their children can adjust to living in two homes, then joint custody is better. Joint custody has the advantage of guaranteeing that both parents stay involved in their children's lives.

Parents who share parenting get more breaks. If they can put their children's interests before their own, they even have less stress. Children feel secure knowing they still have both parents. They have a chance to spend time in each household.

"Spending time with each parent has been great," said Reggie. "I feel like I know both of them really well. And having a change in rules between each house was sort of nice. My dad is more relaxed about how I keep my room and what I eat, while Mom is more lenient about bedtime and curfew."

The experts can't agree on what happens when parents don't get along. Those who favor joint custody say that even with fighting, joint custody is better because children still have lots of contact with both parents. They believe joint custody is fairer; each parent has equal rights. In contrast, experts argue sole custody is unbalanced; one parent has too much authority. Not only is that unfair, but it isn't good for children to see one parent with more parenting rights than another.

The biggest concern is that without any custody, the other parent is more likely to feel too apart from the child, and to fade from the child's life. The fading from a child's life, professionals believe, is worse than fighting.

In contrast, critics of joint custody argue that it doesn't allow parents to be independent of each other. And that need may, in fact, be why they divorced in the first place. Furthermore, if a parent is unreasonable, then joint custody takes away from their child's welfare. It also happens that parents who can't agree often end up in court to settle their disagreement. The concern is that all these bad feelings filter down to the children, who in turn suffer and feel bad. Indeed, many children blame themselves for their parents' fighting, and having that kind of guilt on their shoulders is painful.

Sole custody does give noncustodial parents more time to make a new life. With that time, many adults return to school, take more demanding jobs, or work on other relationships (and themselves). However, for many parents, not having custody is painful and lonesome. They miss their children and feel a great loss in their lives.

Parents whose children visit every other weekend and a few weeks at vacation spend only six to eight weeks a year with their children. This is dramatically less time than most spent with their children during the marriage.

Children, too, feel a great loss. Even though you *know* your parent didn't divorce you, seeing that parent only a day or two a week, or even less, can *feel* as painful as if the parent were gone forever.

Several experts have studied divorced families. Some have found that parents with joint custody get along better and have fewer arguments over money and other issues. But as we've learned earlier, other experts disagree with those findings. The debate goes on.

That joint custody isn't easy or doesn't always work does not mean it isn't worth trying. Giving both parents a chance to remain active parents may make it worthwhile putting up with the hassle of switching homes and even with the fighting that occurs.

Regardless of the kind of custody arrangement you have, it is important to remember that custody measures the time you spend with each parent. In addition, it measures their responsibility toward you. What it cannot measure, however, is how much your parents love you and you love them. Indeed, such measures are beyond the law.

3
GRANTING DIVORCE

Today half the people who marry and say "I do" later divorce and say "I don't." Years ago, divorce was less common. This was not because marriages were any happier, but because divorces were harder to get.

In order to get a divorce, the person who wants it has to prove that he or she has *sufficient grounds* for one. In other words, she has to prove there is an acceptable reason the court should end the marriage.

In the past, divorces were harder to get because it was difficult to convince the court there was enough reason to end the marriage. That's because the only grounds then were if a spouse was guilty of doing something terribly wrong. This wrong was called a *fault*. The most common faults were cruelty, infidelity (cheating on your spouse), drug addiction, frequent drunkenness, or abandoning your family.

The spouse who wanted a divorce had to prove, in court, that her mate had one of these faults. If she couldn't, she would not be granted a divorce.

In 1964, Harry wanted to divorce Sue. He no longer loved her. Sue did not want a divorce. And since she had none of the legal faults, Harry had no grounds for divorcing her.

Harry remained unhappy. He fell in love with another woman. He spent a lot of time with the other woman. But still he had no grounds for divorce. That's because infidelity was his fault, not Sue's. And he wanted the divorce, not she. (Sue would have had grounds for a divorce if she had wanted one.)

Occasionally, in the past, both parents wanted a divorce but neither had a fault. Some couples went to court anyway. There one of them would pretend something like infidelity, in order to convince the judge they had grounds for a divorce. Such pretending was difficult and embarrassing to do in public. Only couples desperate for divorce tried it.

Today divorce is easier to get because we have changed the grounds for divorce. They are more liberal. No longer is fault divorce the only avenue out of a marriage. It has been largely replaced by *no-fault divorce.*

A no-fault divorce is easier to get because you no longer have to prove your spouse has a serious fault in order to have grounds for divorce. Instead, no-fault divorce laws recognize that marriages fail for other reasons. These reasons include living apart (called *separation*), being unable to get along (*incompatibility*), or having too little in common (*irreconcilable differences*), to name a few.

Thus, if Harry wants a divorce today, he can use living apart as grounds. According to state law in Vermont, where he and Sue live, if he moves out of the house for six months, he'll have sufficient grounds for a no-fault divorce.[1]

Not all couples who live apart, can't get along, or have little in common want to get divorced. But those who can't overcome these problems can now use them as grounds for divorce. And since those problems are so common and many people do end their marriage because of them, divorce is common and easier than ever to obtain.

WAYS TO END
A MARRIAGE

Divorce is only one way to end a marriage; other ways are annulment and separation. What all the ways have in common is that one home becomes two. Therefore, no matter how a marriage is ended, if there are children, custody and visitation are always issues to address.

Dissolution
In some states like Ohio, dissolution is the simplest, least expensive way to end a marriage. Together, both partners write an agreement, which they file in court. This petitions—requests—the court to "dissolve" the marriage. Then a judge decides if the agreement is fair. If it is, their joint request is granted.

Annulment
When a couple gets an annulment, they ask the court to treat their marriage as though it never took place. If they have children, then custody, visitation, and child support are awarded. But since there was "never a marriage," *alimony* (support for an ex-spouse) cannot be ordered.

Legal Separation
Some couples don't want to continue living together, but neither do they want a divorce. They may be unsure about divorce or unready for one. Their religion may not allow it, or they may want to stay married for practical reasons like keeping their health insurance or Social Security benefits. These couples can file for legal separation, also called *separate maintenance* or *alimony* only.

Divorce

Divorce remains the most common way to end a marriage. There are three basic kinds of divorce: default, uncontested, and contested. To start any divorce *suit,* the person who wants the divorce files a written *complaint* to the court requesting a divorce. The case is then assigned a number and a judge or referee (someone who helps the judge).

There are legal terms for people involved in law cases. For example, the person starting the procedure is called a *plaintiff,* while the person being sued for divorce is a *defendant.* Together, they are referred to as the *parties* involved.

As soon as a divorce proceeding begins, a judge or referee can award *temporary custody* of the children until the final divorce. This usually goes to the parent who stays with you during the divorce proceedings. If your parents stay together until their divorce is final, they can share custody. Or, if one of your parents is harming you, the court can order that parent to leave and stay away. In that case, the court awards temporary custody to the parent who alerted the court to the danger.

SERVING DIVORCE PAPERS

To give the court *jurisdiction*—control over the case— the defendant must be notified (told) that he or she is being sued for divorce. Getting this written notice is what people refer to when they say, "I was served my divorce papers." If they haven't already hired a lawyer, getting served divorce papers is when most people do hire one.

Vanessa and Bill Clarke were married for ten years. They spent the last seven fighting. When Bill's company transferred him to a different city, Vanessa refused to go with him. After a year of living apart, they agreed to get divorced. Vanessa filed the complaint. But since their divorce was mutual, Bill's lawyer wrote to the court to eliminate having to serve him divorce papers.

In contrast to the Clarkes, the Bonfiglios had not agreed to divorce, though several times Nick Bonfiglio threatened to get one. Sherri was aware of their marital problems, but she was sure that she and Nick could work them out. So when Sherri was served divorce papers, she was surprised. She was also determined not to go along with the idea.

ANSWERING A COMPLAINT

The next step in a divorce procedure is for the defendant to *answer* the complaint. An answer is the legal response to the divorce notice.

Defendants can either ignore their notice or answer it. If they ignore it, however, the plaintiff is automatically entitled to a divorce. Why then, would people choose to ignore their divorce notice?

Default Divorce
Some defendants have left home and can't be found. They can't file an answer since they haven't received notice of their divorce. If a defendant is missing, a notice of the complaint is published in the local newspaper where the court has jurisdiction. (This also means that a parent can take his or her children to a different state and file for a no-fault divorce. The notice of complaint will be published in their new town or city. This makes it unlikely that the spouse will read it.)

Defendants have a certain time period to answer the notice—usually twenty-eight days. If they have not answered the notice by then, the plaintiff is granted a divorce. Such a divorce is called a *default divorce*. Custody can be awarded for default divorce. But not until the defendant is located, can that parent be ordered to pay any financial support.

Uncontested Divorce

All divorce papers include grounds for a divorce. Some, but not all, also include the *terms of the divorce.* (Terms refers to property, support, and custody issues.)

A defendant who receives a notice and agrees to its contents can choose not to answer a complaint. That is because any answer is a protest against the complaint. And the defendant may decide he or she has no protest against it.

Not filing an answer after receiving the notice allows the plaintiff to get a divorce. Such a divorce is called an *uncontested divorce,* since there is no argument against it.

Contested Divorce

Most defendants do answer their complaints. Because any answer is an argument against the notice, the divorce is said to be *contested.*

Even after she was served her papers, Sherri remained optimistic that time and counseling could save her marriage. As a result, her answer "contested" the grounds for the divorce.

Bill Clarke had agreed to divorce. But he wanted to have a *say* in the *terms* of his divorce. He wanted to have a say in who got the house, who got custody of their children, and the like. So Bill's answer contested the divorce also.

In order to get a divorce, these "contests"—or disagreements—must be ironed out first. Until they are, the divorce remains contested and cannot be granted unless a judge settles the disagreements for the couple.

TERMS OF THE DIVORCE

Since this book is already about custody and visitation, following is a brief explanation of the other important issues in divorce proceedings—property and support.

Property Division

Property is what a couple accumulates during their marriage. It also includes any debts they owe, such as charge accounts or mortgages. In order to get divorced, property must be divided and the division must be fair.

Some property is easy to divide. For example, Bill and Vanessa owned a vacation cottage and a speedboat that were of equal value. Vanessa wanted the cottage, while Bill preferred the boat.

Often, however, couples fight over property division. Many people are attached to their home and fight over who gets to keep it. If the couple have built up a business, they fight over how much it is worth. To make property division fairer and easier, many states have come up with formulas for dividing property.

Support

Support is what a court says a person must pay in the future, after the divorce is final (though temporary support is ordered as soon as divorce proceedings begin). There are two kinds of support: *alimony* and *child support*. Alimony goes to an ex-spouse, while child support goes toward raising children.

Alimony may be temporary—for a year or so—or it can last as long as the receiver stays unmarried. Temporary alimony usually goes for tuition to complete an education or for living expenses until an ex-spouse finds a job and can support himself.

Child-support payments go toward your living expenses. Most child support is for food, clothing, and shelter, and also includes tuition, health insurance, and other necessities. It is paid until you grow up and can support yourself. Some children have disabilities that prevent them from ever being self-supporting. These children receive child support as long as they need it.

Today many states have formulas to determine child support. If may be either a percentage of income or a certain amount per month. In many states, the more a parent earns, the more child support he or she is expected to pay.

The cost of raising children is high. Child support rarely covers all of it. And as children grow, the expenses usually increase. Yet in many cases, the amount of child support received doesn't. And, unfortunately, many parents neglect to pay child support at all.

Child Support Is Not the Same
As Custody
Child support is often confused with custody, but they are not the same. It helps to remember that support depends on your parents' income and the cost of raising you, while custody depends on your parents' ability to take care of you and make decisions about you. Therefore, not all custodial parents receive child support. Nor do parents who pay support necessarily have custody, even legal custody. In fact, most don't. And not having custody or as much visitation as they want angers many parents who pay child support.

Sometimes it angers these parents so much, they refuse to pay support. Meredith's mother made it difficult for Meredith to visit her father. She couldn't bear the thought of Meredith being with her ex-husband's new wife and baby. She often kept Meredith away from home—out shopping or elsewhere—when Meredith's dad came to pick up Meredith for visitation. In protest,

Meredith's father withheld his monthly support check.

If visitation is being interfered with, as in Meredith's case, some courts allow parents to withhold their support payments. Similarly, other courts allow parents to keep their children from visiting a parent who refuses, or is late with, support checks. Such tactics, though, victimize children, not just the errant ex-spouse. They deny children contact with parents who truly want to see them, as well as deny the financial support they deserve, and, in most cases, need.

There are other reasons parents don't pay child support. Some honestly can't afford it. Others resent paying support to children they rarely see or have no part in raising. Still others resent paying support when they have no say in how the money is spent.

Since earliest times, there have been parents who failed to look out for their children. Such parents abuse their children or neglect them. Many noncustodial parents are somewhere in between those extremes: they see their children, but seldom. They support their children, but not enough.

Some parents behave as though they divorced the entire family, not just their spouse. Sometimes it's because they were treated the same way when they grew up. Sometimes it's because they feel hurt that their children have turned away from them (which may or may not be so). Still, all parents have a responsibility to their children regardless of the inconvenience, sacrifice, or hostility that entails.

By removing the blame, no-fault divorces are easier to get. What has not been removed, though, is the pain of divorce or the conflicts that come up during divorce proceedings. Formulas make some of these matters easier to settle. But regardless of the changes in divorce laws, custody and visitation remain difficult issues to resolve.

4
REACHING AN AGREEMENT

Only when divorce is uncontested—by default or agreement—can it be granted without going to trial. And because a trial is so costly and disagreeable, most couples do their best to avoid one.

Reaching an agreement can be complicated, especially if there is a lot of property involved. The biggest obstacle, though, is usually anger. Angry parties don't like to give up much. And an unwillingness to compromise is a barrier to success in reaching an agreement.

Another obstacle is our legal system, with its emphasis on winning and losing. Contested divorce suits compel each party to take sides. Taking sides creates opponents. And a spirit of opposition does little to promote compromise or goodwill. In fact, it does a remarkable job of squelching that.

ADVERSARY LAW

Ours is an adversary system of law. Adversarial law is like debating. There are always two sides to every case—a winner and a loser. In order to win, a party must prove that he or she is right and the other side is wrong.

Although they are permitted to represent themselves in court, each side in a divorce suit usually hires a lawyer. Divorcing parties normally hire lawyers with experience in *family law,* a branch of law that includes divorce and custody. Lawyers, or attorneys as they are also called, interpret divorce laws, prepare the case, and present it to the court. It is their duty to do everything legal and honest to win their client's case.

A lawyer can represent only one side in a case. In fact, representing both sides is such a breach of legal ethics that a lawyer can be disbarred for it.

Maxine Jordan is a family lawyer and Beth and Pete McGovern are a divorcing couple. If Ms. Jordan represents Beth, she might try to win for Beth the custody of the children, get Pete to pay as much child support as possible, and perhaps get Beth to keep the house.

In contrast, if Ms. Jordan represents Pete, she will not look out for Beth. Instead she will try to get Pete what he wants. Consequently, if he wants custody, if he wants to pay reduced child support, and if he wants the house, Ms. Jordan will try to get all that for him. Moreover, she will prove why Beth—Pete's adversary in the divorce—doesn't deserve otherwise.

Furthermore, unless it is what her client wants, Ms. Jordan does not have to take into account what the McGovern children want or which parent should have custody of them. After all, what matters to Ms. Jordan is whether or not her client wants custody. Thus, Ms. Jordan's duty is to advise her client what his or her chance of getting custody is. Then, if the client still wants it, she tries to get it for him or her.

Adversarial law might work well for criminal justice cases, but family law is different. Divorce itself is difficult. By making parents take sides against each other, they can lose sight of the important side—their children's. Divorce proceedings are a stressful time. When aggressive lawyers ruthlessly try to win a case, they contribute to turning the whole affair into a war zone and divorcing parents into bitter enemies. The terrible feelings created during such stress take years to heal. By losing sight of the long run, even the side that "wins" in court suffers a great loss.

WORKING OUT AN AGREEMENT

There are many ways couples reach an agreement in order to get a divorce and avoid contest. Some are able to discuss together what they and their children need. Most lawyers, however, advise their clients not to do this on their own for fear that they'll give up something that may be hard for them to get back later.

Many agreements are reached during court "hearings," informal sessions led by a court referee or judge. Others take place in attorneys' offices. Still others occur during *mediation,* which is fairly new in divorce proceedings.

Negotiated Settlement
The most common way to reach an agreement is with a lawyer's help. Lawyers from each side meet with the parties or with each other to work out the terms either during court hearings or in their offices.

In a divorce, it is usually impossible to get everything you want. Lawyers advise their clients to be realistic, to give and take in order to get what they want most. Such legal bargaining is called *negotiating,* while the agreement reached this way is called a *negotiated settlement.*

Partners who feel guilty about their divorce or are in a hurry to get one are often willing to give up a lot. For example, parents may give up custody because they feel guilty about leaving their family. Or they may offer to pay alimony and generous child support to speed up the divorce.

Others will give up something out of fear of losing

what they badly want. Yvonne was so afraid of losing custody that when Mark said he wouldn't fight her on it if she didn't ask for child support, she agreed, even though she needed support money.

When they negotiate, some lawyers take advantage of these weaknesses. This is why negotiated settlements can make enemies out of divorcing partners. It is also why some people don't get a fair settlement. It is the judge's duty to make sure no one gets "taken for such a ride." But judges are busy, and some cases are so complicated that they can't always protect people from unfair divorce settlements.

Mediation

Another method of reaching agreement is *mediation,* whose popularity is growing. Together a couple hires a mediator, who is trained to help people come to an agreement without lawyers. Because a mediator doesn't take sides, mediation is not adversarial like negotiation.

The mediator's job is to help a couple stick to the issues of their divorce and avoid fighting. Mediators sometimes see the whole family together. Because they don't take sides, they can look out for the children.

Even if a mediator has a legal degree, as many do, she cannot give legal advice during mediation. That's because lawyers are supposed to take sides and mediators don't. Critics of mediation say it doesn't let parents work out the complicated financial arrangements of a divorce because mediators don't give legal advice. But supporters point out the large number of people who emerge from mediation with better feelings about their terms. Mediation appears less likely to turn parents into enemies and issues of custody into contests.

Agreements reached through mediation are written into a document called a *memorandum of under-standing.* This is given to lawyers, who draw up a final legal document to file with the courts.

FINALIZING A DIVORCE

The court sets a date for a divorce trial. As long as both parties continue to work on finding an agreement, that date can be postponed again and again. However, if the court date arrives, and one of the parties is pressing to get it over without an agreement, the case must go to the judge. Then a judge will hear both sides of the case, and rule on a divorce plus its settlement.

Reaching an agreement on every term can take weeks, months, and even years. Often it is completed just before the trial is scheduled to occur. Most couples do reach an agreement to avoid going to trial.

Though a referee might handle the case until an agreement is reached, only a judge can legally grant a final divorce. Referees do review cases and pass their recommendations on to judges.

If a divorce is uncontested, the judge will review the formal agreement. He or she may ask some questions. Sometimes a judge insists on a few changes. But since family court judges are so busy, and most believe that parents know what is best for their children, they tend to respect parent's wishes and automatically approve uncontested divorces.

When the agreement is approved, which can take several weeks if the judge needs time to read it over, the final divorce is granted. Afterward, the court will issue final divorce papers.

Through negotiation or mediation, most parents reach an agreement on custody and visitation. Sometimes it's because they really are in agreement. For most people, though, it's a compromise, a way to avoid going to trial.

Divorces may be easier to get today, but divorce proceedings are not easier to go through. Experts once believed that it took only a few years to adjust to a divorce. Now they know that it can take much much longer. Perhaps, though, if parents turned to less adversarial ways, such as mediation, to reach an agreement, some of the pain of divorce would be avoided.

5
CUSTODY CONTESTS

When Kevin's father was served divorce papers, he refused to share custody or give it up. Despite months of negotiation with his wife's lawyer, he would not change his mind. He felt he was a good father and deserved to raise his child. His wife wanted a divorce. She also wanted to raise her child. While going to court to fight over custody was the last thing she wanted, she was not going to give up her child. Nor was she successful in persuading her husband to share custody of Kevin.

As we have learned, most parents succeed at reaching a custody agreement without going to trial. Sadly though, some parents fail to. For their children, this leads to torn loyalties and an uncertain wait to find out where they'll live and who they'll live with. Many children think that the fight is their fault. But children really have nothing to do with it.

Kevin's parents are good parents. Their problem is that angry parents don't always see past their anger. For, unlike judges, parents are not bound by reason. Divorce is a stressful time in their lives. If they are angry, upset, scared, or confused, as many are, they cannot think clearly. They don't always know what is best. Even if they do know, they aren't always strong enough to do what is best, especially if it means a long, drawn-out fight.

According to Phyllis Chesler, author of *Mothers on Trial*, a book about custody disputes, every year there are 25,000 to 100,000 custody contests.[1] Not all fights are over custody—some are over visitation. Nonetheless, these battles drain parents of thousands of dollars in legal fees, not to mention the emotional costs of fighting to keep a child. Nor is the pain over quickly. The trial may last only a few days or weeks. But, according to Dr. Chesler, the average custody dispute takes three years to settle from start to finish.[2] Why the struggle? Why all the fighting?

WHY THERE ARE DISPUTES

Some parents fight for custody out of genuine concern for their children's welfare. They fight to save them from harm like abuse or neglect. They fight to spare them living with an alcoholic or chemically dependent parent. Most fight for custody because they love their children deeply and want to be the parent who raises them.

Unfortunately, many parents fight over custody as a way to hurt the other partner—to "get even." Or they threaten to take custody when what they really want is for the other parent to ask for less child support or alimony. Though it is rare, some parents even falsely accuse the other parent of abuse to deny that parent custody or visitation.

GOING TO TRIAL

Going to trial over custody should be a last resort. It keeps you in limbo, uncertain of your future, sometimes for years. It can be scary and lonely to watch parents fight over you. Despite their spending so much energy and money to win custody of you, during a dispute, it can feel as though they don't really care enough. If one parent tries to turn you against the other parent, it can make you angry too.

Litigation is expensive. Lawyers get paid by the hour and cost hundreds of dollars for a few hours' work. It takes hours and hours to prepare a custody case and take it to court. Many people feel that the money should be spent directly on the children instead.

The biggest cost, however, is emotional. Custody battles make it difficult to be loyal to both parents. By the time you are ten or twelve, your choice of parent carries much weight in court. Consequently, a parent may try to bribe you to choose him or her. Your parent might lavish gifts and promises on you. Or, a parent may threaten you not to choose your other parent.

Children are children, not substitute spouses. They ought not be expected to "fill in for" or "replace" an absent parent. Yet many children are told "you're the man of the house now" or "Take care of your mom." Parents who make children feel guilty about not fulfilling those roles or make them feel lonely or unhappy because they don't have custody, aren't being fair. Children shouldn't have to feel guilty or choose a parent because of it.

Parents are not alone in trying to manipulate a custody battle. Sometimes children bribe or threaten parents as well. When scolded or punished, they threaten to choose their other parent. They may make unreasonable demands on parents who are afraid or are losing custody or who already feel guilty about the effect of their divorce on their children. Their parents' divorce may frustrate, anger, depress, or scare them. Children with those feelings may not realize how they are manipulating their parents or how harmful such behavior is. Sometimes it takes an outsider to point it out to them.

CUSTODY TRIAL

Custody disputes must be settled in court. Usually a referee or judge helps parents (or anyone else fighting for custody) work out a compromise. This can take several hearings. If that fails, then the dispute must be settled through *litigation.* This means going to trial for the judge to learn about the case.

The trial may last several weeks. It depends on how long each side takes to present its case to the judge.

During a custody trial, the adversarial system is set in high gear. Each side tries to make as strong an argument as possible proving they're "right" and the other side is "wrong," and why they deserve custody and the other side doesn't. To do this, each side presents evidence and testimony to support its case. In addition, the sides prepare briefs that cite decisions from similar cases and state laws that support their side.

In addition to the lawyers, courts do their own research. Many staff social workers or psychologists investigate the case and report their findings to the referee or judge.

Basically, each side shows the judge its strong points and the other's weaknesses. The goal is to win custody on your strengths and have the other party lose on its weaknesses.

Strengths include how well your parent takes care of you; how much time he spends with you; your feeling close to him; how likely he is to encourage you to visit your other parent; what kind of home he can provide; and how stable, responsible, and moral his lifestyle is. Other strengths include having grandparents and other relatives on his side who are involved with you. If he has a new spouse or housemate who is supportive of you, that too, is a strength in court.

Weaknesses include proof of the opposite, such as how poorly your other parent takes care of you; how little time she spends with you; how distant you feel to her; how unsupportive she would be of your visiting the other parent; how terrible her home is; and how unstable, irresponsible, or immoral her life-style is. Other weaknesses are proof of abuse, neglect, mental illness, alcoholism, drug addiction, and even remarriage to a spouse who doesn't like children.

Too often, trials focus on the weaknesses and why a parent should be denied custody, rather than on a parent's strengths and why that parent deserves custody.

Information about you is also presented to the judge. This includes how long you've lived with the parent who has temporary custody, how attached you are to that parent, and how well-adjusted you are to your present school and neighborhood. Most important, however, especially if you are at least twelve years old, is which parent you prefer living with.

GUARDIAN AD LITEM

Most custody disputes are hammered out through negotiation or mediation. But if they go to trial, an adversarial approach cannot be avoided. As we learned in Chapter Four, our legal system compels lawyers to look out only for their clients. This means that children in the middle of a custody dispute have no advocate looking out just for them.

To protect children in custody disputes and be their advocates (look out for them), a few states assign a *guardian ad litem* to represent the child in court. (In most states, however, guardians ad litem are assigned only rarely.) A guardian ad litem is someone, usually a lawyer, who is trained in child-custody issues.

Since it is the guardian's role to represent you in

the custody suit, to be loyal to only you, he or she tries to win whatever is best for you.

CUSTODY INVESTIGATION

How an investigation is conducted depends on the expert's training. For example, some experts spend only a few hours on each case, while good ones devote considerably more time and effort. In addition, they usually visit your home and interview not only you and your parents, but also others who know you. In contrast, psychologists or psychiatrists conducting an investigation are likely to interview you and your parents only in the office. They also tend to use psychological tests to learn more about the parties involved.

During a typical court-ordered investigation, an individual hired by the court meets with you and each party fighting for your custody. The person asks many questions and takes notes on the answers. Sometimes you may be asked to write out the answers. (Sample questions can be found in the appendix.)

Some of the questions can make you feel disloyal to one of your parents. For example, a question like: who would you rather have with you in the hospital when you are sick asks you to choose one of your parents. In reality, your answer may actually be: both of them.

The investigator wants to learn how each parent treats you. At one time or other, most children think their parents are too strict or have made mistakes. This is normal. But if someone in your family, including a stepparent or other person, has actually abused you, the investigation is your opportunity to report it.

Other people, referred to as collaterals, may be interviewed. Collaterals include your neighbors, stepparents, grandparents, teachers, and doctors. In addition, some investigators make home visits to see what kind of home each parent can provide. They may also request that your school send them information about you.

After the investigation, the expert writes a report of his or her findings. Some experts give their opinion of how custody and visitation should be awarded. If they find that neither party is capable of raising the children, they report that instead. Good investigators will justify their opinion with sound reasons. They may also be asked to appear in court and testify about their findings and opinions.

WITNESSES

Witnesses are people invited or ordered to court to tell the judge about some (or all) of the people involved in the case. Some witnesses show a judge why a parent should have custody. Others are brought to court to discredit a parent and show why that parent should lose custody, which is said to "damage" that side's case.

When lawyers question their own witness, it is called *examination*. When they question the other side's witness, it is called *cross-examination*.

Mrs. Burgess was the housekeeper for Marshall and Ruth Burger. She was *subpoenaed* (ordered) to court to testify how violent Marshall was to Ruth in front of their children. This was to help prove why Marshall should be denied custody.

Although it happens only rarely, you may be asked to take the stand and testify against one of your parents. What happens normally, however, is that a judge will question you in private. A court stenographer, who records what is said, may also be present. So too may lawyers representing either side. Your parents will not be present, however.

AWARDING CUSTODY

At the conclusion of the trial, each lawyer hands the judge a written brief. This is a summary of what each lawyer showed during the trial. It also cites laws and past decisions that support why each lawyer's client should win the case.

Judges consider what they hear in court. They also read the lawyer's briefs, as well as reports such as the investigation reports. Then they render a decision. The judge alone has the power to make the final decision. It is announced at the conclusion of the trial or a few weeks later.

The award is usually for sole custody. That's because ordinarily, if parents have to go to trial, they will not be able to share custody without returning to court every time they have a conflict. In a few states like California, however, where joint custody is preferred, even parents who fight over custody may be ordered to share it.

6

GRANTING CUSTODY

Maybe you've heard the expression "a King Solomon's case." This refers to judgments that are tough to make, ones that call for great wisdom.

Custody decisions are often King Solomon cases. In fact, in biblical times, King Solomon was called upon to settle a custody dispute. It went like this. Two women lived in the same house. Within a few days of each other, they both gave birth. Each nursed, slept with, and loved her baby.

During the night, one of the babies died. Its mother mourned her loss. Her despair was so great that while her housemate slept, she switched babies, exchanging hers for the one still alive.

When she awoke, the mother with the dead baby in her arms was horrified. This was not just because she was holding a dead baby, but because she was positive that the baby wasn't hers. Then, to her greater horror, she failed to convince the other woman to return her baby.

Their dispute went to King Solomon's court. King Solomon had no way of knowing who the real mother was. So he came up with a clever test. He said to the mothers, "Since there is only one baby and two of you, the baby will be divided by a sword. Then each of you will be given half."

"No!" cried one of the women. "Let her have the baby!" she said, pointing to the other woman.

King Solomon was sure the real mother would rather spare her baby's life than win the dispute. Wisely, he gave the baby to her.

No judge today would use such a drastic threat to settle a custody dispute. Still, when parents fight over custody, judges need as much wisdom as King Solomon to resolve the issue.

IN THE BEST INTEREST
OF THE CHILD

Long ago, children were treated as their father's property. This meant their fathers could put them to work and collect all their wages. It also meant that when fathers divorced, they were entitled to custody.

If a father left the family or was proved unfit, a mother could get custody. Since divorces were often granted for those reasons, women at times did get custody.

By the 1900s, the standard for custody awards shifted from fathers to mothers. Popular was the belief that only mothers could properly care for infants and toddlers—children of tender years, as they were called. Later, the "tender years doctrine" was extended to children up to twelve years of age.

Another belief that grew popular was same-sex custody, based on the idea that children should be raised by parents of their sex. Accordingly, mothers were awarded daughters and fathers were awarded sons.

In 1973, a book written by several leading experts on child rearing was published. The authors of *Beyond the Best Interests of the Child* advised that custody should be awarded to the primary caretaker. This is the person who takes most care of you (primary means "first"). What gender that person is doesn't matter. In fact, to prevent tearing children away from adults they were close to, the authors advised awarding custody even to primary caretakers who weren't the child's parent.

In the past, most mothers stayed home with their children, while most fathers went off to work. Mothers raised the children, fathers brought home the paychecks. Today much of that has changed.

It is common for mothers to work outside the home now. It is also increasingly common for fathers to share the parenting. (In fact, as more fathers do share, the term "mothering" is being replaced by the term "parenting.") Together these changes set new guidelines for custody. They paved the way for both joint custody and more father-awarded custody.

Nonetheless, custody is still awarded in the best interest of the child. Where there is a conflict, judges are supposed to put your interests before your parent's.

Best interests? If it is in your best interest to be raised in a home with a mother *and* a father, then how can any custody decision be in your best interest? For many reasons, the ideal is often not possible. Therefore, your best interest may really be your second best interest or the best choice possible.

HOW JUDGES DETERMINE CUSTODY

It is the judge's duty to look out for *you.* This is true whether your parents reach an agreement themselves or whether the judge has to make a decision for them. Even if your parents come to the judge with uncontested custody, the judge must check it and be sure it is in your best interest. If it isn't, the judge won't grant a divorce until the agreement is improved.

No doubt you and your parents are strangers to

the judge. Furthermore, apart from perhaps being a parent herself, little in a judge's legal training prepares her to be an expert on child rearing. Given both these limitations, how can a judge possibly know what is best?

Years of experience handling custody cases teach many judges what is best. In addition, judges turn to experts like the custody investigators we learned about in a previous chapter.

As we also learned, judges don't have to take the experts' advice. But if experts do a thorough investigation and the judge believes their advice is sound, often they will follow their suggestions. On the other hand, experts hired by only one side may be too biased. Judges prefer experts who can be impartial and look out for what is best for the child, not for the party who hires them.

PREFERENCE

Many referees or judges want to know for themselves how children feel about their custody. Those who are comfortable talking to young people ask to speak with them in private. You can ask them (or they will tell you) if what you say is recorded and whether or not your parents can read it.

What the referee or judge wants to know is if you have a preference for living with one of your parents. (Remember, if your preference is for joint custody, you can share that with them). The judge may already know of your preference from an investigator or guardian ad litem.

In many states, whom you prefer living with is given a lot of weight in determining your custody. In fact, in some states, unless your choice is a parent who is unfit, your wish must be granted. A great deal depends on how old you are and whether you appear to be mature enough to make a decision. As children get older, judges recognize how impossible it is to keep them away from parents with whom they really want to live.

How to decide which parent to choose is beyond the scope of this book (though you may want to look in Chapter Eight for some advice). This subject is probably something you would want to discuss with an adult you respect.

Just as you have the right to make a choice, you also have the right *not* to make a choice. You may be afraid of hurting a parent or feeling guilty in having to choose one parent over the other.

Amanda was asked which parent she wanted to live with. Visiting her father had been fun since the divorce. He was always taking her places like the movies, bowling, skating, and shopping. Yet it was her mother whom she wanted to be with when she was sick, her mother she ran to with her problems. "I love both my parents," she told the referee when asked to choose, "and I could never choose between them."

No parent has the right to pressure, bribe, or threaten you about your choice. Nor does the parent have the right to love you less, punish you, or refuse to see you. Parents who do act this way are hurt or angry. In time, some get over those feelings; others never do. By the same token, it is also your responsibility not to threaten or bribe your parents either.

No matter how your parents act, it is your right as a child not to accept their burden of guilt or blame. If you cannot do that, you may want to discuss this with someone who can help you—a grandparent, school counselor, religious leader, or other adult you trust.

Current Check-Outs summary for FORBOTNIC
Mon Aug 23 16:07:28 EDT 2010

BARCODE: 21701988913
TITLE: Understanding child custody / by
DUE DATE: Sep 20 2010

BARCODE: 21700462354
TITLE: Getting custody : winning the las
DUE DATE: Sep 20 2010

BARCODE: 21704587431
TITLE: The custody solutions sourcebook
DUE DATE: Sep 20 2010

BARCODE: 21704448077
TITLE: May it please the court : courts,
DUE DATE: Sep 20 2010

BARCODE: 21704291161
TITLE: 1-800-DeadBeat : how to collect y
DUE DATE: Sep 20 2010

BARCODE: 21705665177
TITLE: Family law in a nutshell / by Har
DUE DATE: Sep 20 2010

BARCODE: 21703830954
TITLE: CHILD CUSTODY MADE SIMPLE
DUE DATE: Sep 20 2010

BARCODE: 21703833407
TITLE: Fathers' rights : hard-hitting &
DUE DATE: Sep 20 2010

BARCODE: 21704314985
TITLE: Child custody : building parentin
DUE DATE: Sep 20 2010

BARCODE: 21705497922
TITLE: Building a parenting agreement th
DUE DATE: Sep 20 2010

GUIDELINES FOR DETERMINING CUSTODY

Before making their final custody award, judges use certain guidelines or criteria. Most come from what social scientists have learned about children growing up: that having security, stability, love, and discipline are as important as food, shelter, and clothing.

Some guidelines are set by the state's custody laws. For example, some laws will clearly state that custody should go to the parent who has done most of the work raising you. Other state laws are less clear and state only that custody be in your best interests. Still others give no guidelines, letting judges determine custody on their own.

For uncontested custody cases, your parents' wishes, what they agree to, are usually respected. That's because most judges believe parents know what is best for their children.

Contested custody is a different matter. Following are some of the criteria judges use to award custody. Which guideline the judge or referee uses for your custody, if it is disputed, depends on the judge's experience, your state code, and what seems to be in your best interest.

Kind of Relationships with
Each Parent
Courts look at what kind of relationship you have with each of your parents. They want to insure that custody goes to the parent with whom you have the best relationship.

Primary Caretaker Custody is usually awarded to your primary caretaker. This is the parent who takes the most care of you, prepares most of your meals, takes you to appointments, attends your school conferences, and the like. Since your other parent is important, visitation is nearly always awarded to that parent.

Psychological Parent   Courts recognize how important it is for you to be close to the adult in charge of you, so they try to award custody to that person. To determine who it is, they may ask you directly. Or the investigator may discover who it is from questions like these: If you had to be hospitalized, which parent would you want to be with you? (Other questions are found in the appendix.)

The psychological parent is usually the same as your primary caretaker, but not necessarily. You can feel close to a parent you hardly ever see.

*Time to Spend with
the Children*
The judge considers how much time each of your parents can spend with you. He may also look at who has spent time with you in the past; who, for example, has done most of the recreational and educational activities with you.

Parenting Skills
Judges only award custody to fit parents. Fit doesn't mean they can jog five miles or do a hundred push-ups. It means that they are healthy, mature, and capable of raising children. A parent who neglects, abuses, or is unable to care adequately for the children is unlikely to win custody. Such parents may even lose visitation rights.

The judge will also consider each parent's ideas about teaching you values and about discipline, what kind of a home they can provide you, and how likely they are to put your interests before their own.

Mental Health

The mental health of each parent is important. If one has had mental problems requiring frequent hospitalization, for example, the judge or referee might favor awarding custody to the other parent.

Visitation

Since it is important for you to have as much contact as possible with *both* your parents, the judge will favor the one who is least likely to interfere with your visiting the other and, in fact, most likely to encourage visiting.

Stability

Children need stable homes and parents they can rely on. Judges favor parents who can offer stability, who don't move around or change jobs too often.

Life-style

Life-style is difficult to assess. Most judges tend to be conservative about it. They look for life-styles that conform to what they believe is "normal." In deciding custody, a great deal depends on other parenting skills, as well as how the parent compares to the other parent.

Thus, if he can prove he is a good parent, a homosexual parent may still be awarded custody. But many judges refuse to award custody to homosexual parents who flaunt their sexual preference. Likewise, parents who are too open about their dating may not get custody.

Nonparents

As long as parents are fit to be parents, the law recognizes their right to be. Sometimes a well-meaning grandparent or other relative—even a stepparent—may sue for custody. Since custody is a parent's right, unless the parent is unfit or there is a genuine reason to deny custody, most parents win custody fights against nonparents.

This does not mean that grandparents or stepparents cannot get visitation rights. Though not all states recognize a nonparent's right to visitation, more and more do.

Keeping Siblings Together
Years ago, when the custody of daughters and young children went to mothers, and boys and older children to fathers, siblings were often split up. Today judges realize how much brothers and sisters help each other cope with the strain of divorce and they try to keep them together.

This may not always be in a child's best interest, however. John Guidubaldi, Ph.D., a psychologist who has studied the effect of divorce on hundreds of children, advises splitting siblings up if they want to live with different parents. His research suggests that it is better to live with the parent to whom you are closest, even if it means not living with one or more of your siblings.

Other Factors
Many other factors are considered in awarding custody. These include how well you get along with your stepparents, how well you are doing in school, how adjusted you are to your neighborhood, what kind of material comfort a parent can provide, and how much support a parent gets from other relatives like grandparents, aunts, and uncles.

WHEN ALL THINGS ARE EQUAL

When all things are equal—when both your parents are suitable, or, unfortunately, when neither parent is—awarding custody can be a very difficult decision.

Each judge faced with such choices uses different criteria to make a final decision. Much depends on that state's custody code and the judge's own experience. Some judges may favor the parent who can offer more material comfort, while others might favor the parent who has more time to spend with the children. Some judges will decide to grant custody to the parent who seems most likely to encourage visitation, while others will favor the parent who has a bigger support system, such as concerned relatives.

Judges do what they can to make wise decisions about custody. Sometimes the courts are too overcrowded with cases for them to carefully review the uncontested ones. Sometimes they don't get all the facts they need to make the wisest decision.

Major studies about the effects of divorce on children are underway. Each year experts learn more and more about custody. But until we come up with a better system, judges must rely on the guidelines they already have.

7

CUSTODY AGREEMENTS AND VISITATION SCHEDULES

Dan wants to join his school football team. His mother is against the idea, but his father supports him. His parents also disagree about Dan's curfew and his study habits (or what his father calls a "lack of study habits").

Since Dan's parents share custody, they need to work out these conflicts. What steps they are supposed to take to work out their differences are described in their custody document.

The first step is to talk over the situation. Through discussion, Dan's parents did reach an agreement about Dan's homework: the TV had to be turned off by 7 P.M., when Dan had to begin studying.

Talking did not settle the football or curfew disputes, however, so the next step was to negotiate with an attorney. That managed to settle the curfew dispute.

Since football remained a problem, Dan's parents proceeded to the third step: seeking help from a social agency. But despite the social worker's guidance, they still could not agree. According to their custody document, when all previous steps have failed, the final step is to go to court for a hearing and let a referee settle the matter. The referee heard each side, then decided that Dan should be allowed to try football; his mother had to accept the decision.

AGREEMENTS SHOULD BE
STATED CLEARLY

What your parents agree to about custody and visitation is recorded in a written, legal document. Like Dan's agreement, yours may include provisions for settling future disputes. It also includes the most important issues about your custody and visitation arrangements.

Legal documents use very precise words. Being exact makes clear to both parties what has been agreed to, which in turn lessens the chances of misunderstanding. It also makes it easier for referees or judges to resolve future disputes.

For example, to avoid misunderstandings over when your noncustodial parent has visitation, agreements are very specific about what time you get picked up and dropped off, including how many minutes your parent is allowed to be late before he or she gives up the right to a visit on that occasion.

Rather than vaguely saying Lindsay should be returned at "dinnertime," her schedule states she is to be returned by 6 P.M., give or take thirty minutes. That's because if it just said "dinnertime," her mom could take it to mean 5:30 P.M., while her dad might mean 7 P.M. The difference in interpretation could cause worry, anger, and tension for the waiting parent. Though a parent can still be late, by stating the exact time, if a parent is late too often, he or she could wind up in court with a dispute.

Likewise, instead of vaguely saying Lindsay will visit a "few weekends a month" and "on holidays," her schedule states precisely which weekends and holidays: the first and third weekend of every month; Christmas, Easter, and the Fourth of July.

EXAMPLES OF CUSTODY AND VISITATION DOCUMENTS

The following are examples of legal documents. The first is a standard visitation schedule from Ohio. The second is an example of a joint-custody agreement.

These are only samples. Your documents are probably different, to suit you and your parents. Yours may be a sole instead of joint-custody agreement, have more or less visitation, and give different steps for settling disputes.

Reading a legal document the first time can be a challenge. Certain legal terms may be unfamiliar, and the sentences may seem long and awkward. After several readings, though, the words and phrases become easier to read. You can refer to a legal dictionary for further help.

Seeing your own legal documents can help you understand your custody arrangements and visitation schedule. You might ask your parents for a copy. If you don't understand it, ask them to explain it to you.

To protect the privacy of the people who wrote and signed these documents, their names and birthdates have been changed.

Standard Order of Visitation
Summit County Family Court
Summit County, Ohio

1. Alternate weekends from Friday at 6:00 P.M. to Sunday evening 6:00 P.M.

2. The children, and/or the custodial parent, have no duty to await the visiting parent for more than thirty minutes of the visitation time. A parent late more than thirty minutes shall forfeit that visitation period.

3. For the purpose of visitation there are seven holidays as follows:

(1) New Year's Day; (2) Martin Luther King Day; (3) Easter; (4) Memorial Day; (5) Fourth of July; (6) Labor Day; and (7) Thanksgiving. In the odd-numbered years the mother shall have the children on the odd-numbered days and the father shall have visitation on the even-numbered days. In the even-numbered years the father shall have the odd-numbered holidays and the mother the even-numbered holidays.

4.   Each year at Christmas time the custodial parent shall have the children on Christmas Day and the non-custodial parent shall have the children from 1:00 P.M. to 9:00 P.M. on Christmas Eve.

5.   On Mother's Day and Father's Day, no matter whose turn for visitation, the children will be with the appropriate parent on those days.

6.   A two-week visitation each summer, to be arranged for the moment the vacation schedules are posted so that the parties have an opportunity to take the children for vacations.

7.   The child shall celebrate his birthday in the home of the custodial parent, unless it falls on visitation day, and the other parent can make up for the birthday with a separate birthday party if desired.

8.   Visitation does not mean picking the children up and leaving them with someone else.

9.   The residence of the children is not to be removed from the State of Ohio without first obtaining a modified visitation order from the Court of Domestic Relations.

10.   These are the Standard Visitation Rules of the Court, and they will be changed or modified by the Court if it is shown that there is a need for such a change.

Joint Custody Plan of
Dennis and Linda Taylor
(These names have been changed and are fictitious)

We, Dennis Taylor and Linda Taylor, the parents of Lisa, born October 31, 1979, and Scott, born May 3, 1981, do hereby submit this affidavit to the Court of Common Pleas, Summit County, Ohio, Domestic Relations Division, in compliance with Section 3901.04 (1)(D). We present this plan and we propose this joint custody proposal of our two minor children to be solely founded on the principle that the best interest of the children shall be the ultimate and primary consideration at all times. We recognize and agree that no plan, however well conceived, can possibly address itself to all conceivable situations and circumstances that may subsequently arise and accordingly, we recognize fully that it is going to take our individual effort, together with the mutual cooperation in attaining the goals that we have set out for ourselves in this plan, mainly, of trying to make the transition for our children from the one-family home to a two-family home as wholesome, comfortable and beneficial as possibly can be achieved. We mutually declare that we will at all times communicate and discuss and keep foremost in our minds that it is in the ultimate best interest of our children and we sincerely hope that our underlying mutual considerations will result in a successful joint custody plan.

1. The Physical Needs and the Living Arrangements for the Minor Children. *The minor children shall reside with the Father, Dennis Taylor, during the approximate nine months of the school year and with the mother, Linda Taylor, during the summer months. Each of the parties shall be free to select their own residences and each agrees to make the necessary adjustments for*

the living conditions of the children when they are residing with each of the parties. It is also agreed between the parties as part of the plan that Linda Taylor,
the mother, shall during the school year and while the
children are residing with the father, Dennis Taylor,
have the right of visiting on alternating weekends from
Friday after school until Sunday evening, and during
the summer period when the children are with the
mother, Linda Taylor, the father, Dennis Taylor, shall
have the right of visiting with the children on alternating weekends from Friday to Sunday and in addition
thereto each of the parties is granted a vacation period with the children. The mother shall have two weeks
during the school Christmas vacation and one week
during the spring vacation. However, if upon reasonable notice, Dennis Taylor wishes to vacation during
those three weeks it is agreed that the mother, Linda
Taylor, shall be entitled to a period of time equal to the
father's vacation time at such other time during the
school year as the parties shall arrange. The parties
further agree to alternate the major holidays and that
shall include Thanksgiving, Christmas, Easter, Memorial Day, Fourth of July, and Labor Day, and the children shall spend Father's Day with Dennis Taylor and
Mother's Day with Linda Taylor. The parties in compliance with the spirit and the purpose of this joint custody proposal agree to modify the visitation rights set
forth herein as the best interest of the children shall
dictate. The sole purpose of this plan is that the children shall feel the freedom of not being constrained by
fixed and inflexible periods of visitation and it is the
purpose of the parties hereto to develop a feeling of
normalcy and to continue the interest both parties have
in the welfare of their children.

During all the times as said minor children are with
each of the parents herein each party will respectfully
arrange for proper child care and supervision during

any period of time when such party shall be pursuing his or her profession and during all times when the minor children are with either party, the party with whom the children are residing at that moment shall be responsible for the discipline, entertainment, and parenting. However, each party agrees to consult from time to time as problems with the children shall arise. Each of the parties hereto agrees to provide for the cultural and educational enrichment of their children with music, sports, art, dance, and other cultural and educational activities, and the parties shall as best they are able share in the financial cost of these programs together with the decision making process in arriving at what is best for the children. Should one parent determine that he or she prefers a particular type of educational or cultural activity for the child or children and if that parent desires to pay the financial cost thereof, he or she shall be free to do so. It is the agreement of the parties that the children shall attend school from the residence of the father, Dennis Taylor, and the father shall have the right of selecting the residential school facility, and he shall communicate his selections to the mother, Linda Taylor, and it is agreed that the children shall continue to reside in Portage County, Ohio, or possibly in the Ravenna school district. The father, Dennis Taylor, shall select the very best schools for his children and he shall keep in mind the possibility of the children attending a school to which the mother Linda Taylor can easily drive them in the event the children are staying with her during the school year. The children will not be placed in private school institutions unless the parties shall agree mutually at some future date.

It is the objective of this portion of the plan to provide that there shall be as little disruption of the children's lives as is possible and it is the intention of the parties that the children's lives shall not be unneces-

sarily interrupted and that there shall be a free flow of living arrangements coinciding with the normal uninterrupted activities of the children.

2. Financial Matters Involving the Children. *During the time that the children are with each of the parents each parent shall provide a home for the children together with transportation, child care, entertainment, housing and food, and all the necessaries needed by each of the children. The father Dennis Taylor shall be responsible for the major items of clothing and the parties shall consult about these items and each is free to supplement their basic necessities and the basic requirements of each of the children. The father Dennis Taylor shall be responsible for the payment of fifty percent (50%) of the cost of summer camp for the children.*

Medical expenses for the children shall be borne by the father Dennis Taylor except each of the parties is obligated to keep in full force and effect all benefits by way of coverage with their employers, and each shall cooperate fully in paying the medical expenses as they accrue. In the event there are sums remaining unpaid after the application of all benefits of both parents, the father Dennis Taylor shall be responsible for these charges. In the event of a medical emergency each of the parties shall be consulted by the party then having the custody of the children, it being the express desire of the parties to keep each party informed at all times and to cooperate in the ultimate resolution of any medical or dental problems. It is further the agreement of the parties to keep each party informed at all times and to cooperate in the ultimate resolution of any medical or dental problems. It is further the agreement of the parties that although the bulk of clothing and furnishings necessary for the children shall be borne by the father, it is anticipated that the mother Linda Taylor will have additional expenses and in consideration of the fact that the father will be claiming the two children as dependents for income tax purposes, he shall on August 1st of each and every year hereafter as long as he is claiming the children as dependents, pay to Linda Taylor the sum of Two Hundred Fifty Dollars ($250.00) per year as a clothing allowance, to be reduced one-half as child attains the age of 18, is emancipated, or graduates from high school.

3. Conduct of the Parties with Respect to Child Rearing Issues. *The parties hereby acknowledge the significant correlation between parental love for and the discipline of a minor child. Each party hereby agrees that when the children are in their custody they will exercise reasonable parental discretion in all disciplinary matters and they shall from time to time discuss the problems, if any, and their philosophies with regard to their children. Each party further agrees that they will not interfere with the exercise of the other's reasonable parental discipline. They further agree that they will be supportive of the principle that the minor children shall be encouraged to maintain and to foster meaningful relationships with grandparents, extended family members, friends and relatives of each party and all others, and they will discuss and attempt to resolve any conflicts. This plan further intends that the children will be counseled by the parents in a mutually agreeable religious life as the parties shall from time to time agree.*

It is further proposed that in this plan if there should develop any kind of an impasse between the parties on any matter contained in this plan the parties will follow the procedure outlined below in attempting to reasonably resolve the impasse:

1. *The parties will first attempt to work out through compromise and communication to find a reasonable solution by themselves.*

2. *The parties will seek the advice of their attorneys and then the four parties will attempt to work out the problem.*

3. *The parties will secure available community resources such as the Family Service or the Investigation Department of the Domestic Relations Court.*

4. *If all else fails the parties agree to abide by the decision of an impartial mediator or arbitrator selected by them together with their respective attorneys or by reference to the Court.*

4. Future Spousal Relationships and Related Matters. *It is contemplated based on the ages of the children and the parties themselves that the possibility clearly exists that either or both may remarry in the future and it is contemplated and acknowledged by the parties that any such new marital relationship may give rise to the need for adjustments or modifications of this plan. The parties agree that they shall approach the resolution of any future problem in this area with, again, the ultimate obligation of determining what is in the best interest of the children. Each party will notify any future spouses that this plan is in place and is of paramount interest and importance to each of the parties hereto, and should there be any impasses reached the parties agree to follow the procedure set forth herein before until resolution of this impasse.*

This plan is presented and as set forth in the pre-

amble attempts to cover all matters in broad strokes with the recognition that it is almost impossible to anticipate all areas of concern. We do by affixing our signatures to this agreement firmly resolve to make it work and to make it work primarily for the benefit of our two minor children.

Dennis Taylor and Linda Taylor do present this plan and the plan does represent their Joint Custody Plan for their children and they do hereby request the Court to approve the same.

_____
Dennis Taylor

_____
Linda Taylor

STATE OF OHIO)
)   SS:
PORTAGE COUNTY)
SWORN TO before me and subscribed in my presence this _____ day of August, 1983.

_____
Notary Public

Reprinted with permission from Divorce Investigation, Court of Common Pleas, Summit County, Ohio, 1989.

8
MODIFYING CUSTODY AGREEMENTS

Custody is about people. And people change. This is why our laws allow for changes in custody. A change in an original custody decree is called a *modification.* For many reasons, parents and even children seek modifications.

Often modification is for change in visitation. Your noncustodial parent may want to see you more often or otherwise change the visitation schedule. And some noncustodial parents miss their children so much they actually try to get custody.

After a divorce, some parents gain confidence about caring for their children, confidence they lacked at the time of their divorce. With that gain comes the notion they can also gain custody.

When Brigitte's parents got divorced, her mom gave up custody. Because she suffered from depression and had no income, Brigitte's mother felt that Brigitte's dad offered more security and a better home life for Brigitte. A few years of therapy and treatment for depression changed how Brigitte's mother felt. Feeling great, she found a decent job. She remarried. With all this came the confidence needed to raise Brigitte. And so she asked to share custody with Brigitte's father.

Some noncustodial parents try to get custody because they disapprove of the way the other parent is parenting. Or they disapprove of the other parent's dating, housemate, spouse, religious practice, or lifestyle in general.

For those same reasons, some parents who share custody ask for sole custody. Others who are disappointed with their joint custody also ask to change to sole custody. Many who do this are tired of always going to court to settle disputes. Or they find that their children are not adjusting well to the strain of moving between two homes. One judge reported that many couples seeking modification in his court had given up on joint custody within six months of trying it.

If a child is having trouble at home or in school, some parents decide a change in custody might improve the situation.

Jason's mom noticed that Jason was quite withdrawn and moody. He had few friends and the ones he did have were a bad influence on him.

Jason's mom discussed the situation with Jason's school counselor and with Jason's dad. Together they decided to have Jason live with his dad so he could change schools and live in a farming community, which they thought would be better for him.

At first, Jason was nervous. Gradually, though, he learned to like school. His grades improved and he made new friends. It also helped that his mother continued to support him and spend as much time as possible with him.

COMPELLING REASON

The Uniform Marriage and Divorce Act, adopted by many states, gives guidelines for modification. These guidelines discourage changes in custody for at least two years following a divorce, unless there is a good reason, like abuse or neglect. This is to give you a chance to adjust to the change in your family life. It also gives custodial parents security by reassuring them they can raise the child without risking the loss of custody.

Furthermore, to justify a change, most judges insist that it be in your best interest and that there is a compelling reason for it. (Since changes in visitation are usually minor, judges are willing to grant them sooner.)

If switching between homes for joint custody is okay, why is switching custody between parents so bad? The answer is that switching homes involves cooperation and takes place on a regular basis. In contrast, switching custody can be a power struggle. It often involves going to court, and the switch is usually permanent, not temporary.

Since judges are so reluctant to change custody, it is usually easier to get it in the beginning than later. For in the beginning, parents only have to prove they are fit, and most can prove this. Even if there is a custody contest, only one parent has to prove he or she is slightly better as a parent than the other parent. On the other hand, to change custody *after* a divorce, the parent must prove a lot more: it must be proven that the other parent is *unfit,* which is difficult to establish.

CHANGING THE AGREEMENT

Many parents reach informal agreements for minor changes. When Kristin's mom went back to school, Kristin's dad agreed to increase visitation so his ex-wife had more time to study and attend classes. To avoid the expense of lawyers and filing in court, Kristin's parents kept the change informal. However, unless a change is recorded in court, it is not legally binding.

When both parents agree on a change, their lawyers draw up a new document called a modified custody agreement. This agreement is then filed in court where a judge will determine if it is in your best interests.

If one of your parents protests the change, both can go to a mediator or referee for help in working it out. If that fails or isn't available, the parents are left with litigation—going to court and having a judge settle the issue.

RELOCATION

When Dan's parents divorced, Dan's father knew little about taking care of children. That's why he agreed to let Dan's mother have custody.

Although Dan's father had not spent much time with his children before the divorce, afterward he did. He took them every weekend and for a month during the summer.

Soon he was cooking their favorite foods, laundering their clothes, and nursing them when they got sick. Most important, Dan's father felt closer than ever to his children.

When Dan's mother announced plans to marry a man from another state and move there, Dan's father asked for custody of his children. He was afraid that if his children moved away, he'd lose contact with them and the closeness that had grown among them.

The judge listened to both Dan's father's and mother's thoughts about the move. Dan's mother assured the judge her move was not to deny Dan's father contact with his children. Rather it was because her new husband's business was in that state.

Then the judge questioned Dan. Dan told her that he was close to both parents, but that he didn't want to change schools or leave his friends.

Finally, the judge agreed Dan and his sister might

lose the relationship they had gained with their father. But she also recognized that Dan's mother had a compelling reason to move. If Dan's mother still wanted to move, the judge ruled that Dan's father could get custody. This left the mother with a difficult choice: leave her children or ask her new husband to sell his business and move in with her. What compounded the issue was that then her husband-to-be would have to move out of the town where *his* children lived. And while he wouldn't lose custody, since he didn't have it, he would lose frequent contact with his children.

Not all states restrict parents who want to relocate. Some allow custodial parents to move for any reason (except to purposely interfere with visitation). But like Dan's state, many states provide that custodial parents cannot move without consent from noncustodial parents. If they don't get consent, they need a court order to move. And some states are more willing than others to grant such court orders.

Opponents of relocation laws say it denies parents a basic freedom to live where they want. Supporters argue that a child's right to contact with both parents is more important than a parent's right to move, that parenting sometimes requires such sacrifice.

ELECTION

Changes can be initiated by children. Some children ask for a change in custody to get to know their other parent better. Others do it to live with a parent they are already closer to. Still others want to leave a truly bad situation in their present home.

Granting your request for modification is called an election. To make one, you have to be at least twelve years old, and in some states at least fourteen. Unless the parent you choose to live with is unfit, in states allowing elections, judges honor your wishes.

The difference between a preference and an election is timing. Preferences are requests to live with a parent during the divorce proceedings; elections are changes you request *after* the divorce is final, sometimes even years later. Most states allow preferences, but only a few currently allow elections.

The following is Rachael's story of her election.

> When I was twelve, I decided to visit my dad for the entire summer. Mom had remarried years before and I never got along with my stepfather.
>
> Dad's wife had a six-year-old daughter who looked up to me. It was fun having a little sister for the first time ever.
>
> I was happy at my dad's, happier there than my mom's. I thought about that a lot. So one night I told him that when summer was over, I wanted to stay.
>
> "Fine," he said, "if that's what you want, it's fine with me."
>
> I needed to tell my mother about my plan, so I called her on the phone. She said, "It's okay . . . if it's what you want." Of course it was what I wanted. But Mom's voice sounded different, the way it does when she gets upset.
>
> She discussed it with my father. The next day she drove up and took me out for dinner.
>
> At dinner, she repeated what she had told me on the phone, that it was okay to stay if that's what I wanted. I heard her voice say it was okay. But her face looked sad. It didn't seem to agree with what her voice was saying.
>
> Even though she was sad, I still wanted

to try living at my dad's. I looked forward to making new friends, to the excitement of going to a new school, to sharing a room with a sister.

I stayed the whole year. My grades were good, excellent, in fact. I liked school and had lots of friends. And for the first time, I even began attending church.

The only problem was that by now my stepmother didn't seem to welcome me as much as she had at first. In fact, I got more and more uncomfortable being around her. As a result, I started spending more time at my girlfriend's house across the street than I did at home.

I guess my dad was concerned about me. I think he picked up on my unhappiness at home.

At the time, I wasn't seeing much of my mom. While I didn't feel guilty about leaving her at first, now I began to. I guess she was having her own problems because she left my stepdad and was living by herself. My grandmother (my mom's mom) was upset about both of us. Grammy called me and talked for a long time. She told me that I had made a mistake, that I was making my mom unhappy.

I guess because I respect her, my grandmother's remarks got to me. I began feeling real guilty about having left my mom's home.

I decided to call my mom. She had gotten back with her husband and they had moved to a new house. Even though she had never pressured me to visit, and I hadn't seen her much, I began going there more often. And when I was there, I began seeing *how much more comfortable I was there than at my dad's.*

This time I thought a lot about making a change before I told anyone. Besides, I knew I couldn't just keep switching back and forth between my mom and dad.

I thought about how I couldn't get along with my stepmother, how I always seemed to be in her way. I thought about how much I got along with both my mom and dad, but how hurt my mom was that I wasn't living with her anymore.

My relationship with my stepfather remained the same as it had been. He was still too strict. He still expected too much of me. Maybe that was because he is a lot older and had already raised two kids. Maybe it was just his personality. Still, more and more I preferred being at my mom's than my dad's. To me, it just felt more like home. Finally, I decided to move back with my mom.

I wrote my dad a note, telling him that I liked living with him, but I thought it was time to return to Mom. The next morning he was awake at breakfast, which was unusual because he worked night shift and usually slept all morning. My decision was okay with him. "Whatever makes you happy," he told me.

Since it was only a few weeks off, I waited until Christmas and the end of the school semester to move back.

Christmas was good. It was comfortable being with my mom again.

Though I'm sorry she was hurt, I'm not sorry I lived with my dad. It gave me a chance to spend time with him and get to know him better.

BRINGING UP THE SUBJECT TO YOUR PARENT

If you have the opportunity to make an election, you have a duty to make it with maturity and kindness. Try to avoid making a hasty or impulsive decision you may later regret. This means not threatening your custodial parent with election during the heat of an argument, or whenever things don't go your way. For just as you deserve the security of knowing they keep custody of you when you misbehave, parents deserve the security of knowing they can set rules and make decisions without your leaving.

Bringing up the subject of election is not easy, even when tempers are cool. For even though a change may be good, many parents are hurt, angered, or scared by it.

Some children find it easier to inform their parents with a letter or note. Others wait for a quiet time when they are alone with their parent. Still others enlist help from someone else—their other parent, a relative, an adult friend of the family, or a therapist or school counselor.

Don't rely on the parent you leave to be happy about your decision, or even supportive. Like Rachael's mom, she may be tolerant. But if she is afraid of losing you, of being alone, or shows all the reasons parents don't want to lose custody in the first place, she can also act angry, scared, and depressed. While that should not stop you from making an election, it is why elections should be done carefully, after much thought.

Be aware, too, that the law does not allow you to switch back and forth between your parents any more than it allows them to do that to you. If your election doesn't work out, or you prefer living with your other parent, you are entitled to make another election. However, in most cases, that is all the judge will permit you—going and returning.

At twelve, Shane elected to live with his father, who was more lenient about curfew and other rules than his mother had been. Even though he was too young for a driver's license, Shane "borrowed" a sports car and then totaled it in an accident. He got into other trouble as well.

Every time Shane got into trouble, his mother went to court to try to convince the judge that Shane was better off with her. The judge was convinced that Shane was better off with her. But although Shane's father was lenient, the judge did not believe he was truly unfit. Furthermore, the judge recognized how impossible it would be to keep Shane in his mother's home if he was as determined not to stay there as he told the judge he was.

Whether Shane was better off with his father or mother is hard to say. He was closer to his father, but his mother gave him more discipline.

What is important about election is that like joint custody, it gives you a chance for close contact with both parents. That contact may come later than you wanted. It may not work out. And it may not be easy. But like Rachael's, it may be a welcome opportunity.

As we have learned, custody agreements are not written in stone. They can be modified. They can be changed. But neither are they written in disappearing ink. In order to modify them, especially to switch custody, there must be a compelling reason.

9
APPEAL, COURT-SHOPPING, AND CHILD-SNATCHING

Tim's father was frustrated about losing custody. As far as he was concerned, though, he had not exhausted ways of getting it.

Heidi's mother was afraid of Heidi's dad. Even though he had visitation rights, she vowed she'd do everything possible to keep him from Heidi.

Not all parents can accept their custody decree, nor is every parent willing to obey it. Dissatisfied parents like Tim's and Heidi's have several choices. As we already learned, they can modify their custody agreement. Or, as we will learn in this chapter, they can appeal to a higher court to reverse the decision. Both these options are legal.

Out of despair, though, some parents choose to take the law into their own hands. They hide their children from the other parent, then they either file for custody in a new jurisdiction or avoid the courts altogether, choosing instead to stay on the run.

APPEALING THE DECISION

Tina's father lost custody of Tina after a long custody contest. His lawyer was sure the trial had been full of legal mistakes. He advised Tina's father to try to get custody by appealing the case to a higher court.

Our judicial system is like a pyramid. At the bottom

are "lower" courts to handle cases first. Those courts handling divorce cases are called domestic-relations or common-pleas courts.

Stacked on these lower courts are "higher" ones that have a say over the lower court's decision. They can, in fact, overturn a lower court's decision. Such courts are called appellate courts, while the highest of all is called a supreme court.

If a party believes he has a legal reason not to accept a lower court decision, he can appeal to the next court up. That court may turn down his request. If the court agrees to hear it, though, a new trial is held.

Naturally, parents who appeal hope that the new trial will reverse or overturn the initial decision, giving them custody. Appealing does carry the risk that the higher court judge will uphold the lower court's decision instead.

It isn't easy convincing appellate court judges to take on custody cases. That's because appeals take a long time—a year or two. This prolongs the time children have to live with uncertainty, not knowing which parent will get custody of them. Furthermore, if a decision is overturned, it means removing children from a home they are used to living in. By letting the lower court decision stand, judges avoid such stress and instability.

Some cases do get appealed, however. A few go all the way to the state supreme court, though usually only if they need a new interpretation of law.

LOOKING FOR LOOPHOLES IN THE LAW

Parents who are denied an appeal or lose it are left with learning to live with their custody decree. Not all parents can accept this. They feel the court system has been unjust and unfair to them. Rather than go to

the same court again, they look for legal loopholes—
and a new court.

After several attempts to share custody of Kirk, his
father took Kirk and moved to another state. The father
then filed for custody in a new jurisdiction, hoping this
time to win.

Not until after he filed for custody, did the father
inform Kirk's mother about what he was doing. By then,
she had to travel to the new location, hire a new lawyer
there, and go to trial to protest the change. This took
almost a year. By that time, even though the judge
agreed that Kirk's father was wrong to move with Kirk,
he felt it was in Kirk's best interest to let him remain
with his father.

COURT-SHOPPING

Before they file for divorce, either of your parents can
move with you. They may have to wait a certain period
before legally filing for divorce and custody in their
new location. But as soon as they do file, they can get
a temporary custody order. Parents who do this hope
that their spouse won't find them until they've had a
chance to file for temporary custody. The reason it's
legal to move before is that as long as there is no
custody order, either parent already has custody, and
the right to move anywhere they please with their children.

After an order is issued, however, both parents are
required to respect it. They can contest, modify, or
appeal it. But until a new decision is legally awarded,
they must stick with the one they have.

As we have learned, the territory where a court's
power extends is called its jurisdiction. If you live in
Stark County for example, the Stark County Domestic
Relations Court has jurisdiction to handle your parent's
divorce suit.

Each jurisdiction follows the laws of its state. That's because family law is a state, not a federal, matter. It also means there are fifty different divorce codes in the United States. Consequently, the laws vary a great deal.

Because they vary, some people, like Kirk's parents, flee their home state with their children to look for a court where they might get custody. And like Kirk's dad, they rarely give the other parent any advance warning. Moving to change jurisdictions is called *court-shopping* or *forum-shopping.*

In the past, court-shopping was more common. It often got a parent custody. But it also disrupted the child's life, not to mention the despair and frustration it brought to the parent who lost the child. Today court-shopping after the initial decree is rarely successful, because all states have enacted a uniform law to discourage it (called the Uniform Child Custody Jurisdiction Act).

OBEYING THE CUSTODY AGREEMENT

Since it is a legal contract, it's unlawful to disobey a custody agreement. Parents who do so risk losing custody. And since they are in contempt of court (disobeying court orders), they also risk going to jail.

Sometimes parents need to be flexible about their agreement. Getting the flu, for example, is a legitimate excuse not to visit or have your noncustodial parent visit you. But being sick a long time is not. Nor is just about any other long-term reason. Parents with visitation rights, even third parties like grandparents who have visitation rights, are entitled to visitation.

While they are entitled to visitation, however, they don't have to exercise that right. Though the court can order them to pay support against their will, it cannot order visitation. In contrast, while those parents have the right to visitation, children do *not* have a right *not to visit.*

The logic is this: parents have the right to start a new life, even if it means leaving behind their children. And those same parents also have the right to see their children. By insisting that children visit, even against their will, it gives their parents a chance to improve the relationship. (Judges do recognize how difficult it is to make older children, like teenagers, visit against their will.)

If there is reason to believe that a parent can harm or not return you, the judge can order supervised visitation. This is when a third party—usually a social worker—must be present during all visits. In addition, the visits may be restricted to such places as a social agency.

During a supervised visit, the supervisor's presence is supposed to protect the child from harm. The supervisor's other job is to take notes about the visit. Later, if there is a decision to be made as to whether or not to continue supervision or stop visitation altogether, those notes will be reported.

If a parent is too untrustworthy for even supervised visitation, the court can grant a restraining order. This makes it unlawful for that parent to see his children at all.

Making it difficult for a child to visit or keeping a child from visiting altogether is called visitation interference. A parent who interferes with visitation is clearly disobeying the custody agreement. As a result, the other parent can press charges and hold the person in contempt of court.

VISITATION INTERFERENCE

Dr. Elizabeth Morgan was convinced that her ex-husband had sexually abused their daughter. So were many experts who examined the child. Neither Dr. Morgan nor the experts could convince the trial judge, however. He ordered unrestricted visitation rights to the father.

To protect the little girl, Dr. Morgan turned her daughter over to her own parents, the little girl's grandparents. They escaped with her to New Zealand, hiding from everyone, including the judge, the father, and the press.

For her interference and refusal to reveal her daughter's whereabouts, Dr. Morgan was charged with contempt of court. She was sentenced to jail until she decided to cooperate. Because she steadfastly refused to give in, Dr. Morgan remained in jail over two years and her daughter remained in hiding. Only when Congress passed a special bill limiting contempt of court sentencing to twelve months was Dr. Morgan freed.

Some parents flee with their children to protect them from abusive or dangerous parents. Others do it to gain control, though what they gain is not legal custody. Still others do it to get revenge.

Although Dr. Morgan's motive was noble—protecting her daughter—what she did was illegal. Moreover, she was guilty of taking the law into her own hands.

CHILD-SNATCHING

Taking children illegally into hiding is called child-snatching. It is a serious crime.

Dan's father was frustrated. His ex-wife was always making excuses why Dan couldn't go for his visit. But his biggest concern was that his ex-wife would turn Dan against him, talking about what a drunkard and how dangerous he was. Dan's father did drink too much. And there were times when he had lost his temper and struck his wife. But he loved his son and was afraid of losing the boy's affection.

One Sunday, when it was nearly time for Dan to return home, his father got an impulse to keep Dan. "Let's go fishing," he suggested. "It'll be great . . . just you and me."

"What about Mom?" Dan asked. "She's expecting me home soon."

"Don't worry," his dad said, trying to reassure him, "I'll call her and see if it's okay."

Dan was aware that his parents hardly spoke to each other. But he trusted his dad and, besides, a fishing trip sounded like fun.

The problem was that Dan's father never told his ex-wife about the trip. Nor did he inform anyone else.

When Dan failed to return home, his mom called the police. A search was begun and a warrant issued for Dan's father. Not until Dan heard his name on the radio did he understand what had happened.

He felt betrayed by his father—and confused and scared. His father was scared, too. After the news report, Dan's father realized how serious his taking Dan away, even for a few days, had been.

Often we read about children who are abducted by their own parents. According to a survey ordered by Congress in 1988, 350,000 children were abducted by a family member. Like Dan's father, the majority of those parents returned their child to the custodial parent within a week.[1]

And what about the few that didn't return? They remain on the run, moving from place to place, sometimes as often as every few weeks. They change their children's names. They may not even enroll their children in school.

This kind of living takes its toll. As soon as they realize what is happening, children are upset. Some get angry with their other parent for not protecting them from being snatched. Others may appreciate their parent's concern and affection for snatching them, but being on the run is still damaging. And for many, even after a safe return to their custodial parent, there is trouble adjusting—and fear. A fear that may never leave. One man reported that even twenty years after his abduction, he still had daily nightmares about it.

A RECENT CHILD CUSTODY LITIGATION

To deter parents from both court-shopping and child-snatching, a private law-reform group recommended that all states adopt an act they had drafted called the Uniform Child Custody Jurisdiction Act. It was promptly adopted by almost all states.

The difficulty was that a few states refused to adopt the act. As a result, those states became a haven for parents who wanted to re-litigate the custody trials they had lost. To overcome this problem, the U.S. Congress passed a law that is similar to, but not quite the same as, the Uniform Act. The federal law is called the Parental Prevention Kidnapping Act. Both acts discourage parents from forum-shopping, while the federal act also helps parents locate their missing children.

Whenever a parent files for custody in a new jurisdiction, that court must contact the home state court. And unless there is an emergency, the home state continues to have jurisdiction, and its custody decree continues to stand. If parents still want a change in custody, they must do it through the home state court.

To help parents find missing children, the act allows them to use federal and state parent-location services. These include access to computer records of the IRS, Social Security, Department of Defense, and the Veterans Administration. It also includes FBI assistance investigating missing children.

The acts have indeed cut down on court-shopping. What remains is some confusion over which court has jurisdiction in certain cases. The acts have also helped parents locate their missing children. Tragically, it has not stopped all child-snatching.

Court-shopping is a risky way to change custody. For if the "shopper" is found guilty of child-snatching instead, as many now are, they are guilty of a serious offense. In half the states, child-snatching is a misdemeanor, punishable by time in jail. And in the other half, it is a felony, punishable by at least a year and a day in prison. Yet many parents whose missing children are returned will drop charges.

CHILD FIND MEDIATION PROGRAM

Recently a nonprofit organization that has helped parents find missing children started a new program for parents who hide their children called Child Find Mediation. You can reach them by calling their national toll-free hotline, 1-800-A WAY OUT (1-800-292-9688).

Parents in hiding, or their children, are encouraged to call the number. Child Find gives them a chance to work out their conflict through mediation, a method we learned about in Chapter Four. The people who answer the phone call will talk to a parent or child in hiding and explain the program. If that parent wants to try it, a volunteer mediator will contact the searching parent and explain what is going on. Once both parents agree to mediation, they can work out their custody conflict at no cost without fear of being turned over to the police.

*   *   *

Child Find has a new program for child-snatching. By calling their national toll-free hot line—1-800-A WAY OUT (1-800-292-9688)—a parent who has snatched a child (or is thinking about it) can talk to a volunteer mediator. (Children who suspect they have been snatched or are being denied rightful visitation can call as well.) The mediator will help parents resolve their conflict about custody or visitation. The call is confidential and information is not shared with the police or searching parents without the caller's consent.

Accepting a custody decree that seems unfair is difficult. Trying to change it through the courts does not always succeed. Some parents, out of despair, try to change the decree themselves, which can be a crime—one that can send them to jail. Even worse, it is a crime that their children pay for as well with nightmares, insecurity, distrust, confusion, and fear. Children deserve better than that. Fortunately, since few parents do turn to such solutions, most children don't have to suffer from them.

10
LIVING WITH CUSTODY

"The woods would be silent
if only those
birds sang
who sang well."

Being a parent isn't easy. Nor are parents perfect. In fact, if they waited until they were perfect to have children, there wouldn't be many families in this world.

Divorce lets you see, earlier than you might have, that your parents aren't perfect. Parents going through divorce often feel abandoned, betrayed, scared, confused, angry, and sad. And these feelings make it hard for them to be good parents. Moreover, upset parents make mistakes. They may act childish or say hurtful things. At times, they might neglect you or make unreasonable demands on you.

Your parents may have told you that their divorce is best for you, that now there won't be any more fighting or tension at home. Children whose parents have been violent or abusive may feel relieved by divorce. Nearly all children, however, feel sad about it. Most children prefer a family that fights to a divorce. Few children believe divorce is really best for them, however their parents feel about it.

In the beginning of this book, we talked about the fear of losing contact with a noncustodial parent. We have also learned why custody decisions are so difficult to make and why there are rarely clear-cut solutions to the conflicts.

Many children suffer from their parents' divorce. It takes them years to get used to it. Some never accept it. Certainly most children are sad about it. Many are angry, too.

The more contact you maintain with each parent (provided they have not abused you), the better off you are. The challenge of divorce is to recognize that although you may no longer have an intact family, you still have a family. Even though you may get new step-parents and new siblings, your parents will always be your parents. Having both of them involved in your life is very important.

Going through a divorce can be depressing, lonely, tiresome, and stressful. Single parents have the work of two parents. They may complain about how hard their life is: how much it costs to raise you, how tied down they are, how much work they are doing. They may also make more demands on you. They may complain to you about your other parent. They may even fight about you with that other parent.

Hearing all this and watching parents struggle to adjust to their divorce makes many children feel guilty. They also feel guilty choosing a custodial parent.

Feeling responsible for your parents' divorce and even for their unhappiness is common. Feeling guilty is too. But despite those feelings, you must remember *you* did not cause your parents' divorce. No child does. Grownups do all kinds of things children don't like and divorce is one of them.

COPING WITH CUSTODY

There are ways to deal with your feelings about divorce. For example, a way to deal with your parents' arguments is to tune them out. Some children have learned that turning up their radio, sticking their head under a pillow, even hiding in a closet or taking a shower and singing loudly all help mask the sound of parents fighting.

It helps to let out your anger and frustration. Some children can do this with exercise like running, swimming, or push-ups. Some have learned to confide in stuffed animals, even hitting them when they feel the need. And some "confide" their feelings to a favorite pet.

It is not always easy to cope with your bad feelings alone. Talking to someone helps. You can tell your parents what is troubling you. If you can't find a good time to tell them, try writing them a note.

If you don't feel comfortable talking to your parent, find someone else you can trust. Many children find their brothers or sisters have the same feelings, so they share them together. Sometimes, talking to a grandparent, aunt, or uncle, or friend of the family helps.

Jamie's parents were getting a divorce. They did not speak to each other. Yet whenever Jamie was with one parent, he or she probed Jamie about what the other was doing, was dating, or how he or she was spending money—questions like that. Putting Jamie in the middle upset him. It made him angry and confused.

Jamie started stealing. He knew it was wrong, but he did it anyway.

Sometimes children find themselves getting into trouble doing what they know is wrong. Acting like this can be a sign of unhappiness. Jamie was not a bad person getting into trouble. Rather he was an upset child getting into trouble.

Asking for help instead of getting into trouble or letting your problems trouble you shows maturity. It is a smart thing to do. There are also people who are trained to listen to your problems with patience and care. They can help you deal with your feelings and find ways to make your problems easier to manage. These people include school counselors, ministers, priests or rabbis, social workers, psychologists, and psychiatrists.

You can talk to your school counselor or religious leader. Or you can ask one (or both) of your parents to take you to a private therapist. If they won't, try enlisting the help of another adult you trust like a relative, friend of the family, or teacher, someone who could persuade your parents to get help for you.

Divorce support groups are another option. These are groups where children get together with an adult leader to discuss their parents' divorce and their feelings about it. By sharing your thoughts and feelings with others, and listening to theirs as well, you learn ways to cope. In addition, you get support from the group's members.

Many schools and communities have such groups. To find one, again ask your school counselor or religious leader. If there isn't a group in your area, you can start one yourself. With a million children going through their parents' divorce each year, finding members for a support group will not be difficult. Ask an adult you trust to help you. One program, called "Banana Splits," puts out a manual explaining how to start such a group.

"Banana Splits" is a support program for children of divorce. It was developed by Elizabeth Mc-Gonagle for groups of five or more students. Children meet every two or three weeks, usually during lunchtime, to air their frustrations and successes with others going through family changes. A volunteer teacher or counselor guides the discussions and offers individual attention if a serious problem or crisis arises.

To order a Banana Splits manual, send a check or money order for $25 plus $2.00 for shipping and handling to Interact, Box 997, Lakeside, California 92040, or call 619-448-1474.

It is worth your while to keep asking for help until you get it. For no matter how hard it is to ask, it is better than getting into trouble, being depressed, or staying angry. Even with help, your situation at home may not improve. But the way you deal with it can.

STAYING IN TOUCH

Joint custody makes it easier to spend time with both parents. So does frequent visitation with a noncustodial parent. But it is also possible to feel close to a parent you don't see often.

One way to stay in touch with parents you don't see often is by writing letters. Unlike phone calls, letters can be saved and reread whenever you need their comfort.

For those of you who have trouble writing letters, the Write Connection can help.

The Write Connection

The Write Connection (TM) Program is a kit for parents and other adults who are apart from their children and want to stay in touch with them. Except for postage, the kit includes all that is needed to correspond easily with a child on a regular basis. Both parents and children report that the kit has helped them stay in touch with each other.

Two kits are available, one for four- to twelve-year-olds and another for teenagers. To order a kit, send a check or money order for $12.00 to Positive Parenting (TM) Inc., 2633 East Indian School Road, #400, Phoenix, Arizona 85016, or call their toll-free number, 1-800-334-3143. The staff at Positive Parenting will contact parents for you, and explain the program to them.

DEALING WITH REJECTION

Every child wants two parents who love him or her. That's why it's natural to feel rejected and unloved when a parent leaves home and loses touch.

It's important to remember that your parents divorced *each other, not you.* That even an absent parent or a bad parent is still a parent. But parents who don't know how to love themselves probably don't know how to love their children either.

Children who understand why a parent leaves know it isn't their fault. Even so, they feel hurt, angry, and rejected. They may also feel it is their fault for not being "good enough." They may feel unlovable. And if that parent has a new family, they feel replaced and betrayed. These feelings are normal.

Parents who leave are out of your life. But they are never not your parents. Though it is impossible to make up for lost time when they are gone, it may be possible to regain contact with them, even years later.

When Tyler's father left home, he stayed away for three years. Then one afternoon, he telephoned Tyler.

"I was thinking about you," he said, "and thought I'd get in touch."

Tyler was mixed up. His stomach tightened up. He got a lump in his throat. As he held the receiver, his palms grew sweaty.

What should I do? he wondered. I'm so angry with Dad for leaving me. Yet I'm glad to hear his voice again, to know he hasn't forgotten me.

Angry, Tyler slammed down the receiver.

Damn! he said to himself. I should have talked to him . . . gotten his phone number or an address. Now I may never hear from him again.

Such dilemmas have no right answers. Tyler was right to be angry and also right to want a father in his life again. He was right to be afraid of being rejected a second time and also right to want to give his dad a second chance.

If this happens to you, you can tell your parent you need time to think things over. Ask for a phone number or address where he or she can be reached. On the other hand, don't be hard on yourself if you act like Tyler. Such reactions are normal.

It's never too late to change, never too late to be sorry. Though some parents don't change or ever feel sorry, many do. And it would be tragic to miss being with a parent, even if that parent seems to come back into your life long after you needed him. For though you may no longer *need* that person, you can still appreciate each other.

Perhaps you can assure your parent you want to see him again, but that you need to work out your hurt and anger. Or you can tell him you aren't ready to talk now, but maybe later you will be. That way you haven't closed a door forever.

The purpose of divorce for a parent who asks for it is a chance to stop being unhappy. Some people find happiness through new relationships. Others find it through their independence. And, of course, for some the second chance doesn't bring anything better— sometimes it even brings something worse.

In contrast, children don't *ask* for second chances any more than they ask for parents to divorce. Yet many get new stepparents, new siblings, new people in their lives. For some, this brings happiness. For others, it doesn't. Regardless, you grow up anyway. And growing up is a second chance itself.

Custody is the way our society makes sure someone keeps the hearth for you. Visitation is the way we help your noncustodial parent keep another fire going in your life. As we have already learned, noncustodial parents are not nonparents. Just because you no longer live in their house doesn't mean their house is not your home. For home is where the heart is. And a heart is big enough to be in many places.

SOURCE NOTES

Chapter One
1. Thomas A. Nazario, *In defense of children,* New York: Charles Scribner's Sons, 1988, p. 223.
2. Phyllis Chesler, *Mothers on trial,* Seattle, Washington: The Seal Press, p. 78.

Chapter Three
1. Doris Jonas Freed and Timothy B. Walker, "Family law in the fifty states," *Family Law Quarterly,* Winter 1989, p. 386.

Chapter Five
1. Chesler, p. 66.
2. Ibid, p. 75.

Chapter Nine
1. J.C. Barden. "Many parents in divorces abduct their own children." *New York Times,* May 6, 1990.

APPENDIX

The following samples are the kind of questions that a divorce investigator might ask you or your parents (or caretaker). These questions have been written by Mary E. Lindley, M.S.W., author of *A Manual on Investigating Child Custody Reports,* Springfield, Illinois: Charles C. Thomas 1988. Reprinted with permission of Charles C. Thomas, publisher.

Sample Form A

Complete the following questions and give your answers to the investigator.

1. If I were stranded on an island, I would feel best if I were rescued by _____ .

2. If I wanted to have friends stay at my house for a few days _____ would be the most accepting of my friends visiting.

3. If my dad ever got any kind of award, it would probably be for _____ .

4. If my mom ever got any kind of award, it would probably be for _____ .

5. My mom and dad used to have most of their arguments about _____ .

6. The parent who spends more time in activities with me is _____ .

7. The parent who seems the most negative about the other parent is _____ .

8. The parent I have spent the most time with since I was born is _____ .

9. The parent who would be the most likely to take me to a museum or an educational program is _____ .

10. If I wanted to visit one of my parents at a time that wasn't a scheduled visit, the parent who would be the most willing for me to visit the other parent would be _____ .

11. If I wanted to go to a movie and both my parents had other plans, _____ would be the most willing to change plans to go with me.

12. If I were the judge, I would decide that _____ would be the best parent to have permanent custody of me and/or other children.

13. The main reason my mom wants custody is

_____ .

14. The main reason my dad wants custody is

_____ .

15. The parent who seems to consider my ideas and feelings the most is _____ .

16. The parent who has qualities that I would most like to have myself is _____ .

17. The parent I feel most relaxed with the majority of the time is _____ .

Sample Form B

Please complete all the questions below that you can complete without any difficulty.

1) My mom often says that dad _____ .

2) My dad often says that mom _____ .

3) The parent who helps me most with homework is _____ .

4) A book written about my mom would be called

_____ .

5) A book written about my dad would be called

_____ .

6) I like to be treated like _____ treats me.

7) Dad places the most importance on _____ .

8) Mom places the most importance on _____ .

9) _____ has the most patience with me.

10) _____ talks to me the most about topics I am interested in.

11) I would rather spend holidays with _____ .

12) _____ is more willing to take me places that I enjoy the most.

13) My dad's best quality is _____ .

14) My mom's best quality is _____ .

15) The parent who makes me feel the most special and worthwhile is _____ .

16) The parent who says the most negative statements in general is _____ .

17) The saddest I have ever been is _____ .

Sample Form C

Please circle the answer (T for True or F for False) that is the most correct.

T F 1) I have had a bruise, mark or other injury as a result of discipline.

T F 2) I have been touched in places that made me feel uncomfortable.

T F 3) My mom usually doesn't say anything positive about my dad.

T F 4) My dad usually doesn't say anything positive about my mom.

T F 5) My dad would be happier if I didn't want to spend time with Mom.

T F 6) My mom would be happier if I didn't want to spend time with Dad.

T F 7) I feel under the most pressure when I'm with my dad.

T F 8) I feel under the most pressure when I'm with my mom.

T F 9) My dad asks a lot of questions about my visits with Mom.

T F 10) My mom asks a lot of questions about my visits with Dad.

T F 11) My dad should be given custody by the judge.

T F 12) My mom should be given custody by the judge.

T F 13) I have thought at times that life is not worth living.

T F 14) My mom has a problem with drinking alcoholic beverages.

T F 15) My dad has a problem with drinking alcoholic beverages.

T F 16) My dad has hit me in places other than on my buttock area.

T F 17) My mom has hit me in places other than on my buttock area.

Sample Form D

Please complete each sentence with the first ideas that come to your mind.

1) The famous person my dad reminds me of is

_____ .

2) The famous person my mom reminds me of is

_____ .

3) I am happiest when _____ .

4) I am saddest when _____ .

5) My mom becomes the most angry when

_____ .

6) My dad becomes the most angry when

_____ .

7) If I could change one thing about my dad, it would be _____ .

8) If I could change one thing about my mom, it would be _____ .

9) If I were in the hospital and only one parent could stay in the room with me, I would choose _____ to be with me.

10) If I could go to any place I chose for a day and I could only take one of my parents, I would want to go with _____ .

11) The parent who would be the most willing to help me if I got in trouble would be _____ .

12) The happiest time I have had with my mom was _____ .

13) The happiest time I have had with my dad was _____ .

14) The famous person I like best is _____ .

15) If I had $100, I would _____ .

16) I am really looking forward to the day when

_____ .

17) When I get out of school, I would like to

_____ .

Sample Form E

Please respond to those questions that apply to your situation. If your answer includes more than one person, please indicate.

(1) Who prepares your meals?

(2) Who usually selects your clothes?

(3) Who enrolls you in school?

(4) Who takes you to the doctor for appointments?

(5) Who takes you to the dentist?

(6) Who attends school functions such as an open house at school?

(7) Who usually takes care of you when you are sick?

(8) Who takes you to get your hair cut?

(9) Who takes your temperature when you are sick?

(10) Who gives you medicine when it is needed?

(11) Who helps you with your homework?

(12) Who plays with you most of the time?

(13) Who takes you to day care or school?

(14) Who talks to you if you have questions or want to talk about daily activities?

(15)   If you had to be in the hospital for a few days and only one person could be with you in your room, who would you choose to be with you and why?

(16)   Who usually disciplines you when needed?

(17)   Who supervises your daily activities such as your personal hygiene? your recreational activities? your assigned tasks around the house? school assignments?

BIBLIOGRAPHY

Books

Berger, Stuart. 1983. *Divorce without victims.* Boston: Houghton Mifflin.

Bienenfeld, Florence. 1983. *Child custody mediation: Techniques for counselors, attorneys and parents.* Science and Behavior Books.

Chesler, Phyllis. 1987. *Mothers on trial.* Seattle, Washington: Seal Press.

Diamond, Leonard. 1989. *How to handle your child custody case.* Buffalo, New York: Prometheus Books.

Fayeweather Street School. Eric R. Rofes, ed., 1981. *The kids' book of divorce.* Lexington, Massachusetts: Lewis Publishing Co.

Folberg, Jay, ed. 1984. *Joint custody and shared parenting.* Association of Family and Conciliation Courts: Bureau of National Affairs, Inc.

Franke, Linda Bird. 1983. *Growing up divorced.* New York: Linden Press/Simon & Schuster.

Franks, Maurice R. 1983. *Winning custody.* Englewood Cliffs, New Jersey: Prentice-Hall.

Freidman, James T. 1984. *The divorce handbook.* New York: Random House.

Galper, Miriam. 1980. *Joint custody and co-parenting.* Philadelphia: Running Press.

Gardner, Richard A., M.D. 1970, 1983. *The boys and*

girls book about divorce. New York: Jason Aronson.

————. 1982. *Family evaluation in child custody litigation.* Cresskill, New Jersey: Creative Therapeutics.

Glass, Stuart M. 1980. *A divorce dictionary.* Boston: Little, Brown and Co.

Goldstein, Sonja, and Albert J. Sonit. 1984. *Divorce and your child.* New Haven: Yale University Press.

Grossberg, Michael. 1985. *Governing the hearth: Law and the family in nineteenth-century America.* Chapel Hill, North Carolina: University of North Carolina Press: 234–287.

Hyde, Margaret O., and Lawrence E. Hyde. 1985. *Missing children.* New York: Franklin Watts.

Krause, Harry D. 1986. *Family law in a nutshell.* St. Paul, Minnesota: West Publishing Company.

Lansky, Vicki. 1989. *Vicki Lansky's divorce book for parents.* New York: New American Library.

Lindley, Mary E. 1988. *A manual on investigating child custody reports.* Springfield, Illinois: Charles C. Thomas.

Luepnitz, Deborah Anna. 1982. *Child custody: A study of families after divorce.* Lexington, Massachusetts: Lexington Books.

McGuire, Paula. 1987. *Putting it together: Teenagers talk about family breakup.* New York: Delacorte Press.

Mnookin, Robert H., and D. Kelly Weisberg, 1989. *Child, family and state.* Boston: Little, Brown and Co.

Moorman, Thomas. 1979. *How to work toward agreement.* New York: Atheneum.

Musetto, Andrew P. 1982. *Dilemmas in child custody.* Chicago: Nelson-Hall.

Nazario, Thomas A. 1988. *In defense of children: Understanding the rights, needs, and interests of the child.* New York: Charles Scribner's Sons.

Samuelson, Elliot D. 1988. *The divorce law handbook.* New York: Insight Books.

Saposnek, Donald T. 1983. *Mediating child custody disputes.* Washington, D.C.: Jossey-Bass Publishers.

Sussman, Alan, and Martin Guggenheim. 1980. *The basic ACLU guide to the rights of parents.* New York: Avon Books.

————. 1985. *The rights of young people.* New York: Bantam Books: pp. 132–169.

Takas, Marianne. 1987. *Child custody: A complete guide for concerned mothers.* New York: Harper and Row.

Wallerstein, Judith S., and Sandra Blakeslee. 1989. *Second Chances.* New York: Ticknor & Fields.

Woody, Robert Henley. 1978. *Getting custody.* New York: Macmillan.

Articles

Albrecht, Brian E. 1989. Change considered in state law on joint custody. *Cleveland Plain Dealer.* (10 April).

————. 1989. Child custody for dad still uphill battle. *Cleveland Plain Dealer.* (10 April).

Ayres, D. Drummond, Jr. 1988. Judge continues jailing of mother. *New York Times.* (16 December).

Bertin, Emanuel A. 1989. Relocation: No common ground. *Family Advocate.* (Winter):13–14.

Book helps unite mom and daughter after 10 years. 1981. *Publishers Weekly.* (30 October):48.

Budish, Armond D. 1989. Some basic questions and answers on Ohio custody laws. *Cleveland Plain Dealer.* (10 April).

Child custody: What are the options? 1988. pamphlet. Cleveland Heights, Ohio: Divorce Equity, Inc.

Cowell, Alan. 1989. Red tape of two lands in child-custody case. *New York Times.* (31 August).

Freed, Doris Jonas and Timothy B. Walker. 1989. Family law in the fifty states. *Family Law Quarterly.* (Winter):367–528.

Hanley, Robert. 1988. Jersey surrogate ruling down-played by brokers. *New York Times.* (5 February).

Johnson, Dirk. 1989. Struggle for custody of children's faith becomes nightmare. *New York Times.* (11 December).

Kantrowitz, Barbara, et al. 1989. Keeping hope alive: Parents of missing kids must learn to live with "chronic uncertainty." *Newsweek.* (27 November):95–96.

Kutner, Lawrence. 1988. Parent & child: Divorce can be traumatic for adult children, who often feel a profound sense of isolation. *New York Times.* (1 December).

———. 1989. Parent & child: Switching parents for vacation. *New York Times* (10 August).

Leo, John. 1980. Kidnaped by mom or dad. *Time.* (14 July):41.

Lewin, Tamar. 1988. New law compels sweeping changes in child support. *New York Times.* (25 November).

Meyer, Karen Grais. 1986. The child custody evalua-tion. *Behavorial Sciences and the Law.* (Spring): 137–156.

Parent cannot remove child from state. 1989. Wash-ington, D.C.: Newsletter for the National Council of Children's Rights, Inc. (Summer):1,16.

Podell, Richard J. 1989. The role of the guardian ad litem. *Trial.* (April):31–34.

Toufexis, Anastasia. 1989. The lasting wounds of di-vorce. *Time.* (6 February):61.

Wallerstein, Judith. 1986. Children of divorce: An overview. *Behavorial Sciences and the Law.* (Spring): 105–118.

――――.1989. Children after divorce. *New York Times Magazine.* (22 January):19–21, 41–44.

Pamphlets and Reports

National Council for Children's Rights, Washington, D.C.

Friend of the court briefs in support of visitation enforcement. (1985).

Hillery, Alexander G. The case for joint custody. (23 July 1985).

Interview with Elizabeth McGongle, director of Banana Splits, a program that helps children of divorced families in the Ballston Spa, New York, school system. (1986).

Model joint custody bill.

Sixty rapid-fire points in favor of joint custody. (1989).

Ways to end a marriage. Divorce Equity, Inc., Cleveland Heights, Ohio. 1989.

Transcripts

ABC News Nightline: Divorce wars. (18 December 1989).

Oprah Winfrey Show: Custody battles. (27 March 1989).

Oprah Winfrey Show: The shock of your parents' divorce. (16 February 1989).

Phil Donahue Show: Dr. Phyllis Chesler, guest. (1984).

Sally Jessy Raphael: Homosexuals got our kids. (30 November 1989).

INDEX

Divorce (*continued*)
    support groups, 94–95
    terms of, 32–35
Domestic-relations (common-pleas) courts, 82
Dove-nesting, 23
Drug addiction, 46

Election, 75–80
Examination, 48

Family law, 37
Father-awarded custody, 14, 19–20, 52
Fear, 9, 13
Federal Bureau of Investigation (FBI), 89
Forum-shopping, 83–84, 88, 89

Grandparents, 57, 58, 84
Guardian ad litem, 46–47
Guidubaldi, John, 58
Guilt, 25, 44, 54, 92

Home visits, 47–48
Homosexual parents, 57

Incompatibility, 28
Infidelity, 27, 28
Internal Revenue Service (IRS), 89

Investigation, 47–48, 53
    sample questions, 101–111
Irreconcilable differences, 28

Joint custody, 21–22, 24–26, 49, 64–70
Joint legal custody, 22–23
Judges, 40, 48, 49, 52–57, 59, 73–75, 85

King Solomon cases, 50–51

Last Fragment (Carver), 9
Lawyers, 37–39, 46
Legal custody, 13, 18
Legal separation, 29
Legal system, 36–38
Letter writing, 95–96
Life-style, 57
Litigation, 44, 45
Loyalty, 44

Manipulation, 44, 51
Mediation, 38, 39–41, 89–90
Memorandum of understanding, 40
Mental health, 46, 57
Modification of custody arrangements, 71–80
Morgan, Elizabeth, 86

ABOUT THE AUTHOR

Susan Neiburg Terkel grew up in Lansdale, Pennsylvania, and was educated at Cornell University, where she studied child development and family relationships. She has written juvenile books about a broad range of social issues, including *Abortion: Facing the Issues, Should Drugs Be Legalized?,* and *Feeling Safe, Feeling Strong: How to Avoid Sexual Abuse and What to Do if It Happens to You,* which she coauthored with Janice Rench. She lives in Hudson, Ohio, with her husband and three children.

© THE BAKER & TAYLOR CO.